On the title page of the house program and in advertisements in which full production credits are given the following acknowledgments, in not less than 20% of the size of the title, shall be given:

Original Broadway Production produced by
Randall L. Wreghitt   Harriet Newman Leve   Gallin Productions   USA Ostar Theatricals
in association with
Bay Street Theatre   Huntington Theatre Company   Williamstown Theatre Festival

East Coast Premiere at
Williamstown Theatre Festival & Bay Street Theatre
Summer 2000

Originally Produced by Geffen Playhouse
(Gilbert Cates, Producing Director; Lou Moore, Managing Director)
Los Angeles, 1999

HEDDA GABLER was originally produced by the Geffen Playhouse (Gilbert Case, Producing Director; Lou Moore, Managing Director) in Los Angeles, California, on March 16, 1999. It was directed by Daniel Sullivan; the set design was by Riccardo Hernández; the lighting design was by Pat Collins; the sound design was by Jon Gottlieb; the costume design was by Dunya Ramicova; and the production stage manager was Peter Van Dyke. The cast was as follows:

BERTA ............................................................ Marjorie Lovett
MISS JULIA TESMAN ................................. Rosemary Murphy
GEORGE TESMAN ....................................... Byron Jennings
HEDDA TESMAN ......................................... Annette Bening
MRS. ELVSTED .................................. Carolyn McCormick
JUDGE BRACK .......................................... Paul Guilfoyle
EILERT LÒVBORG ............................... Patrick O'Connell

HEDDA GABLER was produced by the Bay Street Theatre, Sag Harbor, New York, in association with Williamstown Theatre Festival (Michael Ritchie, Producer; Deborah Fehr, General Manager) on June 21, 2000, at the Bay Street Theatre and subsequently at the Williamstown Theatre Festival (Sybil Christopher and Emma Walton, Artistic Directors) in Williamstown, Massachusetts, on July 19, 2000. It was directed by Nicholas Martin; the set design was by Alexander Dodge; the lighting design was by Kevin Adams; the original music was by Peter Golub,; the sound design was by Randall Freed (for Bay Street) and Jerry Yager (for Williamstown); the costume design was by Michael Krass; and the production stage manager was Laura Brown MacKinnon. The cast was as follows:

BERTA ................................................ Kathryn Hahn
MISS JULIA TESMAN ........................ Angela Thornton
GEORGE TESMAN ............................ Michael Emerson
HEDDA TESMAN ................................. Kate Burton
MRS. ELVSTED ................................. Katie Finneran
JUDGE BRACK ..................................... Harris Yulin
EILERT LOVBORG ............................ David Lansbury

# CHARACTERS

GEORGE TESMAN — a research fellow in cultural history

HEDDA TESMAN — George's wife

MISS JULIA TESMAN — George's aunt

MRS. ELVSTED

JUDGE BRACK

EILERT LOVBORG

BERTA — the Tesmans' housekeeper

# PLACE

The home of George and Hedda Tesman, Christiania, Norway. Near the turn of the twentieth century.

# TIME

ACT ONE — Morning

ACT TWO — Afternoon

ACT THREE — Early the next day

ACT FOUR — Evening

# HEDDA GABLER

## ACT ONE

*A large drawing room. It is formal, rigid and austere. There is a sofa, some groupings of chairs, a piano and a stove for warmth. Bunches of flowers are everywhere. Too many — as though they had accumulated over the past day or so and reached saturation point. French doors lead off the drawing room to a verandah, which gives out on a garden just on the cusp of changing from autumnal reds and ochers to wintery grays and blacks.*

*At the rear of the drawing room, a doorway leads to a small library. It is dominated by a painting of an old man in a general's uniform. This picture does nothing to elevate the sense of conviviality in this house. Milky Scandinavian morning light filters in through the French windows.*

*Berta enters, flustered, with yet another bouquet. She looks around for somewhere to put it, settling finally on the piano. She then begins to remove the dust cover from a chaise when the doorbell rings. She hurries off and we hear muted greetings from offstage. Miss Tesman enters, followed by Berta.*

MISS TESMAN.  Oh, they're not up yet!
BERTA.  That's what I was saying, Miss Julia! You know how late the boat got in last night! And Mrs. Tesman had to unpack every last thing before she'd go to bed!
MISS TESMAN.  Well, then let's let them sleep. But when they

do get up, won't they love this fresh morning air…? *(She crosses upstage right and opens the drapes, the sheers and the windows.)*

BERTA. *(Picking up Mrs. Elvsted's flowers.)* Oh, there's no space left for any more of these — *(She sets them on the piano.)*

MISS TESMAN. So now you have a new mistress, Berta dear. God knows how hard it was to let you go.

BERTA. Oh, miss! For me too! All the years I've been with you and Miss Rina …

MISS TESMAN. Berta, please. Let's both try and be calm about it. Because we know it's the right thing — George needs you here.

BERTA. But I just keep thinking about Miss Rina, lying there, sick at home! Helpless — and that new maid? — She'll never learn how to take care of an invalid!

MISS TESMAN. I'll train the maid, and what I can't train her to do, I'll do myself. Please, you mustn't worry about my poor sister. We'll all be fine. We'll all cope.

BERTA. The thing is … I'm just … I'm so afraid I won't be able to please Mrs. Tesman.

MISS TESMAN. Well, it might not be easy at first, but —

BERTA. I can tell she's very particular —

MISS TESMAN. Yes, but she's General Gabler's daughter! Think what life with him must have been like. Remember seeing her riding with him? In that long black cape, that giant feather in her hat…?

BERTA. I know — but I never thought she'd end up marrying our little student.

MISS TESMAN. Berta. You can't call George a student anymore — It's Dr. Tesman now.

BERTA. That's exactly what Mrs. Tesman told me. So it's true?

MISS TESMAN. Isn't it wonderful? They made him a doctor! I only found out last night at the pier.

BERTA. Well, I always knew he could do anything he set his mind to, but I never thought it would be medicine.

MISS TESMAN. No, no, darling, not that kind of doctor. Anyhow, you'll have something much more important to call him than "Doctor" pretty soon.

BERTA. Oh? And — What is that, miss?

MISS TESMAN. Wouldn't you like to know. Oh … if only my

poor brother could look up from his grave and see how well his little boy has done! Berta, why are you taking the dust covers off the furniture?

BERTA. Mrs. Tesman told me to. She said she couldn't stand them.

MISS TESMAN. They're going to use this as their living room?

BERTA. That's what she said. *(Tesman crosses stage right, upstage in the library. He sees Aunt Julia.)*

TESMAN. Aunt Julia!

MISS TESMAN. Good morning! — Good morning!

TESMAN. Dear Aunt Julia — all the way out here — and so early in the morning! Wonderful!

MISS TESMAN. Well, I had to see how you were doing.

TESMAN. But — You couldn't have gotten much sleep, Auntie.

MISS TESMAN. Oh, I don't need — who cares about that?

TESMAN. You got home safely from the dock?

MISS TESMAN. It was all fine — the Judge saw me right to my door.

TESMAN. I'm sorry we couldn't give you a ride. But you saw for yourself how much luggage Hedda had.

MISS TESMAN. Yes, amazing ... All that luggage.

BERTA. Should I go see if I can help Mrs. Tesman?

TESMAN. No thanks, Berta — I wouldn't bother her just yet. If she needs you, I'm sure she'll ring.

BERTA. All right then ...

TESMAN. *(Handing her the suitcase.)* But you could take this with you, if you would?

BERTA. I'll put it in the attic. *(She exits into the library. He closes the doors behind her.)*

TESMAN. That entire case, Auntie, was filled with copies I made of the most unbelievable documents. Just lying around in archives! Things nobody knows about — forgotten details — lost little bits of utterly vital minutiae.

MISS TESMAN. So, in other words, you didn't waste any time on your honeymoon, did you, George?

TESMAN. Not a second. Auntie — come on — take off your hat, let me undo the bow for you ...

MISS TESMAN. Oh, it's like you were still at home with us.

TESMAN. Huh — what a pretty little hat you've bought yourself.

MISS TESMAN. Yes, well — because of Hedda.

TESMAN. Hedda? What do you mean?

MISS TESMAN. So she wouldn't be ashamed of me if we were seen walking together in the street.

TESMAN. Oh. Aren't you — ? You think of everything, don't you, Auntie? *(He places the hat on the stage left chair at the center table.)*

MISS TESMAN. Oh. I can't tell you: It is so good to have you home! Jochum's little boy — Look at you! Look at you —

TESMAN. And I'm just as happy to see you, Aunt Julia. You know you've always been like a mother *and* a father to me.

MISS TESMAN. Oh, I know you'll always be fond of your old aunts.

TESMAN. What about Auntie Rina? Is there any improvement?

MISS TESMAN. Oh no. We can't expect that. We have to live with it: her lying there. That's what it is now. I just hope God lets me hold on to her for a little while longer. Because — I really don't know what I'd do with my life, George. Especially now that I don't have you to take care of anymore. I —

TESMAN. Now, now, it's okay; there — there — shhhh.

MISS TESMAN. No, but to think of it! It's amazing — you're married — and to Hedda Gabler! Who used to be surrounded by men dancing around her —

TESMAN. I know! And I imagine there are several gentlemen in this town who are absolutely green with envy right now, eh? No?

MISS TESMAN. And then to have a five- — almost six-month honeymoon —

TESMAN. Well, I mean, strictly speaking — I was working too. All those archives to pore through, and all the libraries. All those books …

MISS TESMAN. Oh, I'm sure it was all work — *(She takes a seat downstage on the chaise.)* George, is there anything special you have to tell me?

TESMAN. From the trip — ?

MISS TESMAN. Yes.

TESMAN. I've told you everything. I got my doctorate. But I told you that last night.

MISS TESMAN. Yes, no, I know that, but are there any prospects for...?

TESMAN. Prospects ...

MISS TESMAN. Expectations! George — I am your aunt, after all.

TESMAN. Of course I have prospects, Auntie — Certainly!

MISS TESMAN. You have?

TESMAN. Of course! I expect to be made a full professor any day now.

MISS TESMAN. Ah, yes, a full professor.

TESMAN. You know that, Auntie.

MISS TESMAN. It's true. I do. But — We were talking about your trip — it must have cost a lot of money, George...?

TESMAN. Yes, quite a bit. But the fellowship helped cover most of it.

MISS TESMAN. Well, I can't see how you could make that stretch for two ...

TESMAN. Quite a feat, isn't it?

MISS TESMAN. And traveling with a lady — presumably that's so much more expensive?

TESMAN. Quite true. But Hedda had to have that trip. There was no way around it.

MISS TESMAN. It seems more and more the thing to do these days — everyone has to have a honeymoon abroad — but George — tell me! Have you examined your new house yet?

TESMAN. From top to bottom. I've been up since dawn.

MISS TESMAN. And?

TESMAN. It's delicious. It's exquisite. And you've arranged it all so beautifully.

MISS TESMAN. Oh, George, do you really think so?

TESMAN. It's simply splendid. I'm a little stymied over what to do with the two rooms between the study and Hedda's bedroom, but ...

MISS TESMAN. Well, George. My dear boy, don't you think time will present a solution to that particular problem?

TESMAN. Absolutely. As my library grows and expands —

MISS TESMAN *(Cutting him off.)* Exactly. As your library grows. That was exactly my thinking.

TESMAN. The thing I love most about this place is knowing how much Hedda always dreamt about owning it. She used to say, "The thing I want most in the world is to live in Senator Falk's villa ..."

MISS TESMAN. And then to have it come on the market ...

TESMAN. We've been exceptionally lucky, haven't we — ?

MISS TESMAN. Yes. But George, dear — it's all going to be expensive. All of this ...

TESMAN. I know, yes, no, I know, it is ... yes. Oh dear. Is it?

MISS TESMAN. Oh, dear God, George, you do realize that. Don't you?

TESMAN. Well. How much? Roughly...? Speaking? A wild guess.

MISS TESMAN. I wouldn't know where to begin until I've seen some of the bills.

TESMAN. Of course! But — the good news is that Judge Brack has gotten us an exceedingly fair deal. At least, that's what he wrote to Hedda.

MISS TESMAN. Don't worry about it, dear. And as for the new furniture — I've been able to put up some security for it —

TESMAN. Aunt Julia — What kind of security could you give?

MISS TESMAN. I took out a mortgage on our pensions.

TESMAN. What? On you and Aunt Rina's *pensions?*

MISS TESMAN. Well, I couldn't think of anything else to do.

TESMAN. But that's — Are you crazy? You live on that! That's all you live on!

MISS TESMAN. Now, now. Don't worry about it. It's just a for-mality. Judge Brack explained it all — he arranged the whole thing — and he said, "It's just a formality."

TESMAN. Yes, fine, but —

MISS TESMAN. And you're going to be getting a salary of your own now. So, good Lord — so what if we have to give you a hand as you're starting out — nothing could give us more pleasure. Nothing.

TESMAN. It just seems there's no end to how much you'll sacri-fice for me.

MISS TESMAN. George. My darling boy — it is a joy for me. My only — to smooth the way for you a little? After all — you haven't had parents to turn to. Have you? But here we are — finally at our goal! And after some very black times too, which, thank God, you've seen your way through.

TESMAN. Yes. It's amazing how it's all sort of worked out ...

MISS TESMAN. And the ones who were against you, and tried to block your way — have all fallen. Collapsed! Yes! And who fell the hardest? The most dangerous of them all. And now he has to lie in his own filth — a wrecked creature ...

TESMAN. Uhm, what do you mean? Have you heard anything about Eilert? Since I left, I mean?

MISS TESMAN. No. Just that he's supposed to have published a new book.

TESMAN. Really? Well — what — ? Eilert Lovborg? Is this ... a recent — ?

MISS TESMAN. It seems to be. But God knows there can't be much to it, right? No. But when your new book comes out, that'll be a different story, won't it? What'll it be about?

TESMAN. It's all about the domestic handicrafts of Brabant during the Middle Ages.

MISS TESMAN. Really! Imagine! That you can write about such a thing!

TESMAN. Well, it's going to be a while before it comes out. I have so much material to sort through first, and to organize. Collate ...

MISS TESMAN. Yes. Sorting and organizing. You have such a talent that — You really are my brother's son.

TESMAN. I'll tell you — I'm looking forward to getting started. Especially now that I have my own home to work in.

MISS TESMAN. And above all, now that you've gotten the wife you had your heart set on, darling. That's the most important of all.

TESMAN. Yes, you're right, Aunt Julia, Hedda. Hedda is the most wonderful thing that has ever happened to me. A blessing. A salvation. Yes. She is. *(Hedda opens the library doors and enters.)* Oh Hedda, dear — good morning! How are you?

HEDDA. Good morning, Miss Tesman. Visiting us so early — that's so very ... kind of you.

MISS TESMAN. Did the bride sleep well in her new home?

HEDDA. Yes. She did. Reasonably soundly.

13

TESMAN. Reasonably? You were — when I got up you were sleeping like a log!

HEDDA. Luckily, yes. But you know how it takes time to get used to the new, Miss Tesman. Little by little. Small steps. Eh? Oh, this sunlight? That maid's left the verandah door open — The light is so glaring in here.

MISS TESMAN. Well, let's close it. *(She crosses to the window to close it.)*

HEDDA. No, just the curtains. That's right. It gives the room a softer light. *(Miss Tesman closes the sheers.)*

TESMAN. Yes, exactly — now you can have both shade and a breeze.

HEDDA. Well, that we need. These flowers are all very — pungent — aren't they? But — please — won't you sit a while, Miss Tesman?

MISS TESMAN. No, thank you, now that I know everything is fine here, I have to run. My sister is just lying there, waiting for me, poor thing.

TESMAN. Give her my love, Auntie, and tell her I'll be by later to see her.

MISS TESMAN. Of course — and I almost forgot — I have something for you — *(She crosses to the desk and picks up the wrapped package.)* Look. *(Miss Tesman hands the package to Tesman. He unwraps it to reveal his slippers.)*

TESMAN. Oh my God. You kept them for me! It's unbearably touching! Hedda ... look at these!

HEDDA. What is it, dear?

TESMAN. My old house slippers!

HEDDA. Ahh! Right. You referred to them more than once on the trip —

TESMAN. Well — I missed them so much! Here — look — now you get to see them, Hedda!

HEDDA. No, thanks, I really don't —

TESMAN. Can you imagine — Auntie Rina lying there, embroidering them — as sick as she was. Oh, God, they bring back so many memories —

HEDDA. Uhm. Yes. I can see that. But not for me.

MISS TESMAN. I do see her point, dear.

14

TESMAN. But now that she's part of the family —
HEDDA. George, this maid isn't going to work ...
MISS TESMAN. Berta?
TESMAN. Why not, dear?
HEDDA. Look. She's left her old hat just sitting out on a chair.
TESMAN. But Hedda —
HEDDA. What if someone came in and saw this?
TESMAN. But Hedda — it's Aunt Julia's hat!
HEDDA. Is it? It is? Oh.
MISS TESMAN. Yes, and it's brand-new, Hedda.
HEDDA. I guess I didn't really look at it very carefully, Miss Tesman.
MISS TESMAN. It's actually the first time I've worn it out.
TESMAN. It's a beautiful hat! It really is. Magnificent. Has such a —
MISS TESMAN. George. It is a very ordinary hat, is what it is. Now, what did I do with my parasol? Because that's mine too ... not Berta's.
TESMAN. A new hat! A new parasol! Extraordinary, right, Hedda?
HEDDA. Both so delightful. Really. Charming.
TESMAN. Exactly! And speaking of delight — isn't Hedda — Auntie — take a look at her — isn't she — ?
MISS TESMAN. George, darling. Hedda has always been beautiful. That's not new ...
TESMAN. I know that, but look at how she's filled out while we were on the trip!
HEDDA. Please — no — don't —
MISS TESMAN. Filled out?
TESMAN. You can't quite see it in this dressing gown, but I, who have had the opportunity —
HEDDA. You haven't had any opportunity for anything.
TESMAN. It's probably that Tyrolean mountain air that makes —
HEDDA. I'm exactly the same as when we left.
TESMAN. You keep saying that, but you're really not. Auntie — don't you agree?
MISS TESMAN. Beautiful. She is beautiful, beautiful, beautiful. God bless and keep Hedda Tesman. For George's sake.

15

HEDDA. Oh. No, let me go ... I ...

MISS TESMAN. And I won't let a day go by without looking in on the two of you.

TESMAN. Please, of course, Auntie.

MISS TESMAN. Goodbye. Goodbye. *(Miss Tesman exits. Tesman sees her out. Hedda crosses downstage center, clenching her fists. She crosses up to her father's portrait and kneels before it. She bows her head to him, rises and paces upstage. She ends at the windows. She violently closes the drapes and then opens them again. This moment past, she leans against the wall and stares out the window. Tesman enters stage left.)*

TESMAN. What are you looking at, Hedda?

HEDDA. I'm just looking at the leaves. They're so yellow. And withered.

TESMAN. Yes. September. Already ...

HEDDA. Already September.

TESMAN. I thought — Did you think that Aunt Julia was a lit-tle odd just now? Sort of ... overly formal? Do you think something's bothering her?

HEDDA. Well — I barely know her. Isn't she always like that?

TESMAN. Not really. Not like today.

HEDDA. Maybe it was the thing with the hat?

TESMAN. It might have been, but — for just a moment —

HEDDA. But the manners — I mean — to toss your hat on a chair? It's just not done.

TESMAN. Well, she won't do it again. I can assure you.

HEDDA. If I did anything — I'll try and make it up to her ...

TESMAN. Yes, dear Hedda. I wish you would.

HEDDA. When you go to see them later, why don't you ask her over this evening.

TESMAN. Yes. I will. And there's one more thing you could do to make her unimaginably happy.

HEDDA. Oh?

TESMAN. If you could just — if you could stop calling her "Miss Tesman" and call her by her first name.

HEDDA. No, Tesman. I told you before. Please don't ask me to do that.

TESMAN. For my sake, Hedda.

HEDDA. I'll try to call her "Aunt" ... And that's the best I can do. *(Beat.)*
TESMAN. Yes, yes. All right. It's just that now you're part of the family —
HEDDA. Hmn. Maybe. I don't really know ...
TESMAN. Is there something wrong, Hedda?
HEDDA. I'm just looking at my old piano. It really doesn't fit in with all this, does it?
TESMAN. Uhm, well — with my first paycheck, we'll see about exchanging it for a new one.
HEDDA. No, I don't want to do that. I don't want to exchange it. We'll move it into this room. And then, when we can afford it, put a new one in here.
TESMAN. Oh. Uhm. Yes, why not? That would be fine. We could do that.
HEDDA. These flowers weren't here last night.
TESMAN. Oh. Maybe they're from Aunt Julia.
HEDDA. A visiting card. "Will return later in the day." Guess who this is from.
TESMAN. I don't know. Who?
HEDDA. Mrs. Elvsted.
TESMAN. Really? That's — Miss Rysing, wasn't it? Before she married some rural provincial commissioner somewhere...?
HEDDA. Exactly. You know who she is. She had very irritating hair. Which she was absurdly proud of. I was under the impression that she was an old flame of yours.
TESMAN. No. Yes, uhm — but it was before I knew you! And it didn't last very long at all! I wonder why she's here. Amazing!
HEDDA. I think it's odd that she would want to see us. I haven't seen her since school.
TESMAN. I haven't seen her in a million years. She's stuck out in the middle of some backwater ...
HEDDA. Listen, Tesman, isn't he — Eilert Lovborg, isn't he living up around there too?
TESMAN. Yes, I think, in the area. *(Berta enters.)*
BERTA. The lady who came earlier, ma'am — She left the flowers you're holding — she's back.
HEDDA. Oh, is she? Well, show her in. *(Berta exits into the hall-*

17

*way. Mrs. Elvsted enters stage left, followed by Berta. Berta closes the doors after her.)* How are you, my dear Mrs. Elvsted! How lovely to see you again!

MRS. ELVSTED. Yes — it's been a long, long time, hasn't it?

TESMAN. Very. For us too. Far too long!

HEDDA. Thank you for the beautiful flowers.

MRS. ELVSTED. Oh, don't mention it. I wanted to see you yesterday, but I heard you were just getting back from a long trip —

TESMAN. So, you've, uh, just arrived in town — ?

MRS. ELVSTED. Yesterday afternoon. I was so upset when I heard you were away.

HEDDA. Upset? Why?

TESMAN. Why, Miss Rysing? — I mean Mrs. Elvsted —

HEDDA. There's nothing wrong, is there?

MRS. ELVSTED. Yes, there is. And I have no one here to turn to but you.

HEDDA. All right, sit here.

MRS. ELVSTED. I can't sit, I'm too anxious to —

HEDDA. Of course you can. Sit here. Right next to me.

TESMAN. Now, tell us what's going on with you, Mrs. … Uhm …

HEDDA. Has something happened at home?

MRS. ELVSTED. Yes. And no — Please, I don't want you to misunderstand me —

HEDDA. In that case, Mrs. Elvsted, just say what's on your mind!

TESMAN. After all, uhm — that's why you came, right?

MRS. ELVSTED. Yes, of course. It's that — if you don't know this already — Eilert Lovborg is also back in town.

HEDDA. Lovborg is here?

TESMAN. Really? Amazing! Yes? Lovborg is back? Hedda — my God! Did you hear that?

HEDDA. Yes, of course I heard her. I'm sitting right here.

MRS. ELVSTED. He's been here about a week already, and this town is so dangerous — so unhealthy for him, and I know he's mixing in all that bad company —

TESMAN. Oh, no …

HEDDA. But, may I ask — what does that have to do with you?

MRS. ELVSTED. Oh, it's — he works for us. He's been the children's tutor.

HEDDA. Your children?

MRS. ELVSTED. No. My husband's.

HEDDA. Stepchildren.

MRS. ELVSTED. That's right.

TESMAN. But — was he — was he stable — I suppose is the word — enough ... uhm? To teach children?

MRS. ELVSTED. In the last two years, his behavior has been exemplary.

TESMAN. Really? That's extraordinary. I mean — did you hear that, Hedda?

HEDDA. I did.

MRS. ELVSTED. Above reproach. In every way. But being here in this city — with money in his pocket, I'm terrified of what might be happening.

TESMAN. But why didn't he stay up there? With you and your husband? Eh?

MRS. ELVSTED. When his book came out, he became more and more restless. Distracted. He just couldn't settle —

TESMAN. Yes, Aunt Julia told me he had a new book out.

MRS. ELVSTED. It's magnificent. A cultural history of Western civilization. And it's becoming something of a sensation. People are talking about it — it's everywhere you go.

TESMAN. Is it? And — and — and it's something he had in a drawer from ... better days, right?

MRS. ELVSTED. You mean the old days, don't you?

TESMAN. Exactly.

MRS. ELVSTED. No. He wrote it all up there in the country. With us. In the past year.

TESMAN. Isn't that marvelous? How surprising — Hedda — can you imagine that?

MRS. ELVSTED. Now — if it would only last.

HEDDA. Have you seen him since you got to town?

MRS. ELVSTED. No, not yet. I had so much trouble finding out where he's staying. It took me till this morning.

HEDDA. Do you mind if I say I find it odd that your husband has —

MRS. ELVSTED. My husband? What do you mean?

HEDDA. Odd that he sends you on this errand. That he sends

19

you to look after his friend. Instead of coming himself. I don't understand that.

MRS. ELVSTED. Oh, no. My husband doesn't have time for — and I had some shopping to do as well, so —

HEDDA. Ah, yes. Shopping. Well, in that case ...

MRS. ELVSTED. Please, Mr. Tesman, I beg you — I know Eilert Lovborg will try to see you. Please be kind to him. You were such good friends. And you're both in the same field, aren't you?

TESMAN. Yes, we were working on similar tracks, once.

MRS. ELVSTED. So, I'm imploring you — both of you. Please, would you promise me that you'll keep an eye on him? ... See that he doesn't start ...

TESMAN. Of course! With only the greatest pleasure, Mrs. Rysing...!

HEDDA. Elvsted.

TESMAN. I'll do everything I can for Eilert. You can count on it.

MRS. ELVSTED. Oh, you're such a kind man — thank you so much — ! Because he means so much to my husband. *(Beat.)*

HEDDA. Tesman. You should write to him, I think. Give him an opening. Or he might be too hesitant to come on his own.

TESMAN. You're absolutely right, Hedda. That's probably the most useful way, don't you think...? Eh? A note.

HEDDA. Yes. And actually, you would want to do it as soon as possible. Right now, really.

MRS. ELVSTED. Oh, please, if you could, that would be so — !

TESMAN. Uhm — I'll do it this instant, if you'll give me his address, Mrs. ... Elvsted.

MRS. ELVSTED. Yes. Here. *(Hands him a slip of paper from her bag.)*

TESMAN. All right. I'm going to do it — just as soon as — *(He looks around the room.)* As soon as I find my damn slippers ... *(He finds them on the desk.)* Here we go, all set...! For the writing of notes, eh? Yes! *(He exits.)*

HEDDA. Tesman. Make sure it's a nice, warm, chatty letter, will you? Bring him up to date.

TESMAN. *(From offstage.)* Yes — that's exactly right!

MRS. ELVSTED. But please don't say anything about my asking you to!

TESMAN. *(Returning from the library.)* Oh. But naturally. That goes without saying! Doesn't it? Hmn? *(Tesman exits again into the library. Hedda closes the double doors.)*

HEDDA. Now then. Here we are. We've killed two birds with one stone, haven't we?

MRS. ELVSTED. What do you mean?

HEDDA. You couldn't tell I wanted him out of the room?

MRS. ELVSTED. Yes. To go write the letter.

HEDDA. Of course. But also to get a chance to talk to you alone.

MRS. ELVSTED. About all this?

HEDDA. Exactly.

MRS. ELVSTED. But Mrs. Tesman, there's nothing more to say. That's it.

HEDDA. Oh, no. There certainly is. A great deal more. That much is very clear. Now. Come. Sit here ... And we can have a nice talk. And be completely candid with each other.

MRS. ELVSTED. But really, Mrs. Tesman, I have to go.

HEDDA. Oh, you can't be in that much of a hurry. Don't you want to tell me a little bit about your life at home? I do want to know.

MRS. ELVSTED. That's the last thing I want to talk about.

HEDDA. But you can talk to me! My God! We were at school together, after all.

MRS. ELVSTED. Yes, I remember. You were ahead of me, and I was so terrified of you.

HEDDA. Terrified of me! No!

MRS. ELVSTED. Yes! You used to pull my hair whenever we met on the stairs ...

HEDDA. I did? Really? No ...

MRS. ELVSTED. Yes. And once you threatened to burn it all off.

HEDDA. Oh, come now. That was just girls being silly —

MRS. ELVSTED. Well, I was very stupid back then. And we've moved in such different worlds, haven't we? In just the opposite direction from each other.

HEDDA. But we should take this opportunity to reconnect! Because back in those days we were very close!

MRS. ELVSTED. I don't remember ever —

HEDDA. Yes, of course we were. And that's why we should be

21

able to talk freely now. *(Beat.)* So, look: No more "Mrs. Tesman."
Please. It's Hedda.

MRS. ELVSTED. Your kindness is — I'm not used to people
being so sweet to me —

HEDDA. Now, now, now, and I'm going to call you Thora. Just
like at school.

MRS. ELVSTED. It's Thea.

HEDDA. Yes, yes. That's what I meant. So, you're not used to
kindness, Thea? Not even in your own home?

MRS. ELVSTED. But it's not my home. It never was and it never
will be.

HEDDA. I thought it might be something like that.

MRS. ELVSTED. Yes, yes. It is.

HEDDA. And ... Am I remembering this correctly? You went up
to the country to be the commissioner's housekeeper?

MRS. ELVSTED. I was governess. At first. But Mrs. Elvsted, the
first Mrs. Elvsted, that is, was so ill. She was in bed most of the
time. So I had to take care of the house too.

HEDDA. And then, finally, it was your house.

MRS. ELVSTED. Yes. That's right.

HEDDA. Huh. How long ago was that?

MRS. ELVSTED. That I got married? Five years ago.

HEDDA. Yes. It must be.

MRS. ELVSTED. Oh, God. These last five years, the last three in
particular, Mrs. Tesman, if you only knew —

HEDDA. "Mrs. Tesman"? Thea, I told you —

MRS. ELVSTED. Oh! I'm sorry, I'm trying ... Hedda. If you
only knew —

HEDDA. Eilert Lovborg has been up there for ... what? About
three years or so?

MRS. ELVSTED. Eilert Lovborg? Yes. That's right.

HEDDA. Did you know him before? When you still lived here?

MRS. ELVSTED. No, not really. Just by name, of course.

HEDDA. But when he moved up to the country, he would visit?

MRS. ELVSTED. Every day. He was teaching the children.

HEDDA. And of course your husband — he must be gone a lot
of the time?

MRS. ELVSTED. As commissioner, he has to cover the entire

district. So, he's never there, Mrs. — uh — Hedda.

HEDDA. Thea. Tell me everything.

MRS. ELVSTED. I don't know how to talk about — If you ask me questions, I can — *(Beat.)*

HEDDA. Is your husband a good man? Does he treat you well? Are things — ?

MRS. ELVSTED. I suppose he means well.

HEDDA. He's much older, isn't he? Because, that can't be an easy thing.

MRS. ELVSTED. There's twenty years between us. And it's true: We have nothing in common, we —

HEDDA. But he's fond of you, at least — ? In his own way?

MRS. ELVSTED. Is he? I couldn't actually tell you. I'm inexpensive. I don't cost a lot to keep.

HEDDA. That was your first mistake.

MRS. ELVSTED. Yes, but it's true: I'm useful to have around. But he doesn't think of anyone but himself. Maybe he has some feelings toward his children, but —

HEDDA. And feelings for Eilert Lovborg.

MRS. ELVSTED. Eilert Lovborg? Why do you say that?

HEDDA. Well, I mean. Here you are. Looking for him. And you told Tesman you'd been sent to look for the man.

MRS. ELVSTED. Is that what I said? I don't ... *(Beat.)* Well. I might as well tell you: It's going to come out sooner or later —

HEDDA. Thea dear — ?

MRS. ELVSTED. The long and the short of it is: I've left. And my husband doesn't even realize it.

HEDDA. He doesn't know you're gone?

MRS. ELVSTED. He's away. Oh, Hedda. I just couldn't stand it anymore. Being up there, so completely alone for the rest of my life.

HEDDA. So what now?

MRS. ELVSTED. I don't know. I just quietly packed up as little as I could and I walked away.

HEDDA. Just like that? It's very brave.

MRS. ELVSTED. I — I didn't look back. I just got on the train and came to town.

HEDDA. What will happen when you go back?

MRS. ELVSTED. Go back? No. No. I'm never going back.

HEDDA. You mean — You're leaving your marriage?

MRS. ELVSTED. There's nothing else to do.

HEDDA. But what will people say?

MRS. ELVSTED. Whatever they like. All I've done is what I had to do.

HEDDA. So now what? How will you live?

MRS. ELVSTED. I have no idea. All I know is that if I am going to live, it has to be near Eilert Lovborg.

HEDDA. Thea. How did you and Lovborg become friends?

MRS. ELVSTED. Oh, gradually. Little by little. I think I started to have an effect on him.

HEDDA. An effect?

MRS. ELVSTED. A kind of power, I suppose.

HEDDA. Oh, yes?

MRS. ELVSTED. And he began to slowly change. The old habits. *(Beat.)* Not because I asked him to. I'd never do that. He just saw that it upset me and stopped.

HEDDA. So, in other words, you saved him, did you? Thea?

MRS. ELVSTED. That's what he says. And in return, he taught me to use my mind, and to start thinking.

HEDDA. Sort of a teacher to you too, right?

MRS. ELVSTED. He talked to me. About everything. And when he wrote something, we'd work on it together.

HEDDA. True comrades, were you?

MRS. ELVSTED. Yes! Comrades! Exactly! That's what he said! And I know I should be happy, but I'm so scared it's not going to last.

HEDDA. Don't you have more faith in him than that?

MRS. ELVSTED. There's something standing between Eilert and me. One of the women from his past.

HEDDA. Who?

MRS. ELVSTED. I don't know. Someone he's never forgotten.

HEDDA. What's he told you about her?

MRS. ELVSTED. Nothing. Just a vague reference once —

HEDDA. Tell me what he said!

MRS. ELVSTED. When he left her, she tried to shoot him with a pistol.

HEDDA. Oh, that's got to be nonsense. People don't really do that.

MRS. ELVSTED. No. That's why I think it has to be the red-headed singer that he was always seeing for a while —

HEDDA. Yes. It very well could be.

MRS. ELVSTED. Because I remember they used to say she walked around with loaded guns all the time.

HEDDA. Well. Then it must've been her.

MRS. ELVSTED. Yes, but Hedda. I've heard that she's back in town. And I'm so anxious about it ... *(Tesman is heard offstage.)*

HEDDA. Shh! Thea — all this has to stay just between us.

MRS. ELVSTED. Yes! My God. Of course! *(Tesman enters from the library, handing a letter to Berta and giving her mailing instructions.)*

TESMAN. I've done it. And Berta has sent it off.

HEDDA. Great. And Mrs. Elvsted was just leaving. I'm going to see her out. *(She starts to exit. Judge Brack enters from offstage left. Berta crosses upstage of the doors just as he has entered and closes them.)*

BRACK. May one presume to call on you so early?

HEDDA. One may presume.

TESMAN. You're always welcome here, Judge. Judge Brack — Miss Rysing.

BRACK. Ahh! A pleasure.

HEDDA. It's really so rare and so delightful to see you in day-light, Judge.

BRACK. Do I seem ... different?

HEDDA. Well, maybe you look a little younger...?

BRACK. That is exceedingly kind of you.

TESMAN. But what about Hedda? Isn't she blooming? She's filled out in the most remarkable way —

HEDDA. Stop it. You should be thanking the Judge for having gone to so much trouble —

BRACK. Nonsense! It was a pleasure!

HEDDA. No, you're a good friend. Let me just see my other good friend out and I'll be right back. *(Mutual goodbyes. Mrs. Elvsted follows Hedda out.)*

BRACK. So. Is your wife happy with everything?

TESMAN. Yes, of course; we can't thank you enough! There are a few things here and there that we've got to rearrange, a few things missing, apparently, which I suppose we have to buy —

BRACK. Really?

TESMAN. But Hedda says she'll take care of it. Why don't we sit down.

BRACK. Well, I only have a moment. I want to discuss something with you actually, Tesman. If I may?

TESMAN. Uh-oh. Now comes the serious part, is that it...?

BRACK. No, no, no. There's no rush for us to get into the dreary financial details. Though I suppose I wish we'd been a little more fiscally ... conscious in setting all this up.

TESMAN. Yes, I know, but how? You know Hedda — you know her better than almost anyone. What was I supposed to do — offer her a little apartment somewhere on the edge of town?

BRACK. No, exactly. That's precisely the problem.

TESMAN. Well then, fortunately, it can't be too long before I get my promotion.

BRACK. Well, these things tend to sort of drag themselves out.

TESMAN. Do you know something?

BRACK. Not really. Nothing finite. But — incidentally — you know your old friend Eilert Lovborg is back in town.

TESMAN. Yes. I already know.

BRACK. How?

TESMAN. The lady who just left with Hedda told us.

BRACK. Oh. Right. I didn't quite catch her name.

TESMAN. Mrs. Elvsted.

BRACK. Ah. Yes! The wife of the commissioner. Right! Lovborg was holed up near them.

TESMAN. It's great to hear that he's sort of on his feet again, don't you think?

BRACK. Yes. They say he's pulled himself together.

TESMAN. And come out with a new book.

BRACK. He has indeed.

TESMAN. Which has created a bit of a sensation.

BRACK. A very big sensation, actually.

TESMAN. Isn't that amazing? You know — he had such a talent — I was certain he'd squandered it and was in perpetual free fall.

BRACK. We all thought that.

TESMAN. But the big question has got to be — what can he do?

How will he make a living? *(Hedda reenters.)*

HEDDA. Tesman is always worrying about how people are going to survive.

TESMAN. Good Lord — it's poor Eilert Lovborg we're talking about here!

HEDDA. Oh, really? Is he in trouble?

TESMAN. He must have run through his inheritance a while ago. And you can't exactly write a new book every year — Can you? No. So, I was asking what's going to happen to him.

BRACK. Well, funny you should mention that. Because maybe I can shed a little light.

TESMAN. Uh-huh.

BRACK. You must remember that his family has a great deal of influence.

TESMAN. Yes, but they washed their hands of him.

BRACK. Right. And he was the white shining hope for that family. Their golden boy.

HEDDA. Who knows? Some people get many chances in life. He's been rehabilitated, apparently, up at Commissioner Elvsted's. A new man.

BRACK. And published a big book. So —

TESMAN. Right. So maybe people will see their way toward opening their hearts to him again. Well. I've just written to him, inviting him over tonight.

BRACK. But, Tesman, did you forget — ? You're booked — Tonight's my little stag party — I told you last night at the pier.

HEDDA. Did you forget, Tesman?

TESMAN. Completely! Good God! Yes.

BRACK. Well. Lovborg won't show up here. I can assure you.

TESMAN. Why do you say that?

BRACK. Listen. My dear friends. I do have to tell you something.

TESMAN. What, Judge? Is it about Eilert?

BRACK. Both you and him.

TESMAN. Well, then just tell us.

BRACK. All right. I think ... Your promotion is not quite the foregone conclusion one hoped and wished for.

TESMAN. Has something gotten in the way?

BRACK. I would think that there's now some competition for the

27

post, yes.

TESMAN. Competition! Do you mean — Judge — with…?

BRACK. Yes. Exactly. Eilert Lovborg.

TESMAN. No. This is unthinkable. It's unbelievable!

BRACK. Nevertheless.

TESMAN. But Judge. It would be so … completely … inconsiderate — at the very least — toward me. Eh? I mean — I'm a married man! Hedda and I got married on the prospect of that promotion — ! Ran up debts! Borrowed money from Aunt Julia! Because that job was practically promised to me!

BRACK. I'm sure you'll get it, but it's going to involve some very rigorous competition, and it's always better to know these things sooner rather than later.

HEDDA. Yes. Just think, Tesman. It'll be sort of like a duel. Won't it?

TESMAN. I don't know how you can be so amused by this, Hedda!

HEDDA. I'm not. I'm actually extremely eager to know how it all turns out.

BRACK. In any case, Mrs. Tesman, before you start buying treasures for this place, I wanted to tell you.

HEDDA. Oh, yes, but this doesn't change anything.

BRACK. Well then. *C'est la guerre. (To Tesman.)* I'll come and get you on my way home this afternoon, all right?

TESMAN. Yes, please — sorry — I don't know where I'm at right now. I'm in such a fog.

HEDDA. Good-bye, Judge. And come again soon. Will you?

BRACK. Thank you. Good-bye now. *(Judge Brack exits.)*

TESMAN. Oh God, Hedda. This is exactly what happens when you let your fantasy life run away with you! Isn't it?

HEDDA. And … Is that what you've done?

TESMAN. Hedda! I'm not deluding myself here — I've been living in a dream world — getting married and setting up a home — based on nothing but expectations, not actual reality!

HEDDA. That might be very, very true.

TESMAN. Well. At least we have the house we always wanted, right, Hedda? This is real. This house we dreamt of living in, eh? Right?

HEDDA. We did agree, didn't we, that we were going to have a particular kind of life? A social life? Entertain, have parties, did we not? That was the bargain.

TESMAN. Yes! God yes, and I was looking forward to that! You — as a hostess — society — yes, yes, yes. But — but now — it's going to have to be just the two of us — at least for a little while! I mean — we'll have Aunt Julia over now and then. I know this isn't exactly what you had in mind ...

HEDDA. And of course, I'm going to presume that a butler is no longer realistic. Correct?

TESMAN. Oh, my! No. No! It's out of the question. For now.

HEDDA. And the same goes for the horse you promised me?

TESMAN. Horse? My God! Hedda! For riding?

HEDDA. I know. I should put that right out of my head. Eh?

TESMAN. Good God in heaven, yes, please!

HEDDA. Well, at least I have one thing left to amuse myself with.

TESMAN. Thank goodness! What is that, Hedda?

HEDDA. My pistols, of course, George.

TESMAN. Hedda. No!

HEDDA. Yes. General Gabler's pistols. Exactly.

TESMAN. Oh, please, Hedda, darling. Don't play with those things, for God's sake. They're dangerous! For my sake, Hedda — !

# ACT TWO

*The piano has been moved into the library, and in its place is a writing table. The flowers are all gone, except for Mrs. Elvsted's bouquet. Hedda enters from the library, a pistol in her hand. Its twin sits in a case on the writing table. Hedda walks around the room, taking aim at various objects. She looks outside and smiles, pointing the revolver out the French door toward something in the garden.*

HEDDA. Well, hello again, Your Honor!

BRACK. *(From offstage.)* Likewise, Mrs. Tesman.

HEDDA. *(Standing back and taking aim out the window.)* And now, your honor, I'm going to shoot you.

BRACK. No-no-no! Don't point that thing at me!

HEDDA. That's what comes of sneaking in through the back. *(She fires the pistol.)*

BRACK. Are you crazy!

HEDDA. Uh-oh. I didn't hit you, did I?

BRACK. Enough!

HEDDA. All right, Judge, come on in. *(Judge Brack enters through the window and crosses to Hedda. He has changed his clothes and is dressed for a party.)*

BRACK. Do you mind? *(He takes the pistol away from Hedda.)* Christ, Hedda, you're still playing with guns? What're you shooting at?

HEDDA. The sky. Just the blue sky.

BRACK. *(Returning the pistol to its case, he smiles wistfully, examining it.)* This thing. Oh, yes, we remember you, don't we? There we go. Tucked away in your little case. Look, let's not have any more of that kind of fun today, okay?

HEDDA. Well, what do you want me to do with myself?

BRACK. Haven't you had any exciting visitors?

HEDDA. No one. Everyone we know is still in the country, I guess.

BRACK. And Tesman is out?

HEDDA. *(Taking the pistol case up to the library.)* At the Aunties'. He skittered out right after lunch. He didn't think you'd come for him so soon.

BRACK. Yes, that was stupid of me; I should have realized.

HEDDA. Why stupid?

BRACK. Because if I'd been thinking, I'd have come earlier.

HEDDA. Oh. Well, then you'd have been sitting here all by yourself. I've been up in my room, getting dressed, since lunch.

BRACK. And isn't there a little peephole in the door we could have talked through?

HEDDA. That, my dear Judge, you forgot to arrange.

BRACK. Also stupid of me.

HEDDA. Well, we'll have to just get settled in and wait for Tesman, won't we? He's going to be out for a while, you know.

BRACK. I can be patient.

HEDDA. Well?

BRACK. Well?

HEDDA. I asked first.

BRACK. All right, then, let's have a nice, cozy little chat — Mrs. Hedda.

HEDDA. It feels like forever since the last time we had a good talk.

BRACK. Every day you were gone, I'd walk by here and wish you were home.

HEDDA. Believe me, so did I.

BRACK. Really? I thought you were having the time of your life.

HEDDA. You have no idea.

BRACK. But that's what Tesman wrote in all his letters. "Time of our lives."

HEDDA. Of course he did, because nothing makes him happier than rooting through old documents in dusty libraries and making endless copies of things. Parchments, or whatever they're called.

BRACK. Well, I mean, yes, that is his life, to some extent. Isn't it?

HEDDA. Right, that's true, so if that's your life, then — oh — but God, what about me? I've been so insanely bored!

BRACK. Really? Seriously? Have you...?

HEDDA. *Think* about it! To go six months — six whole months — without running into anyone you know? Nobody who could talk about what's going on back home? Our circle, our crowd? Nothing!

BRACK. Yes. That would be very hard.

HEDDA. But the worst of it is —

BRACK. What?

HEDDA. Just to be with the same person without a break —

BRACK. *(Nodding.)* Right. Morning, noon and night.

HEDDA. Without even the smallest break! At all! Always and forever.

BRACK. Yes, yes. But our good friend Tesman is so —

HEDDA. My dear Judge: Tesman is an academic specialist.

BRACK. This is true. Yes.

HEDDA. And let's face it: Academics just aren't all that much fun to travel with. After a while.

BRACK. Not even the academic specialist one loves?

HEDDA. Ugh. Please don't use that sugary word.

BRACK. You're joking.

HEDDA. Well — you try it. You try listening to the "cultural history of Brabant," morning, noon and night.

BRACK. Always and forever ...

HEDDA. Exactly! And, my God, all this about the "domestic craftwork in the Middle Ages"? It's a nightmare.

BRACK. Excuse me, but, if all that is true, how did you ever — ?

HEDDA. Conclude that George and I would make a good match?

BRACK. Right. Yes. You could put it that way.

HEDDA. Is it really that strange?

BRACK. Well, yes and no, Hedda. *(Beat.)*

HEDDA. I had danced my last dance, my dear Judge. *(Beat.)* My time was up. Ugh! I can't say that. I can't even think it.

BRACK. You certainly have no reason to.

HEDDA. No, no. Reason. Right. *(Beat.)* And Tesman is a very respectable choice.

BRACK. Respectable. Dependable ... absolutely solid.

HEDDA. And there isn't anything that's literally ... ridiculous about him. Is there?

BRACK. Ridiculous? No. I wouldn't say that, no.

HEDDA. Yes. And he's an extremely devoted scholar, isn't he? So there's every chance he might make a name for himself. Right?

BRACK. Exactly. *(Beat.)* But ... I'm sorry. But actually — I thought you shared everyone else's opinion that Tesman was going to shine very brightly. Eventually.

HEDDA. Yes, I did. So then, when he pursued me so ... avidly, so hungrily, I thought, "Well, fine, then. Why not?"

BRACK. Of course. From that perspective, I can see —

HEDDA. And it was certainly more than my other admirers were willing to do, dear Judge.

BRACK. Well, I can't speak for any of the others. But as far as I'm concerned, I've always had a certain respect for the bonds of matrimony. In a general sort of way.

HEDDA. Oh, I never held out any hopes for you. Believe me.

BRACK. Hedda. All I want is to be of service. You know? To a close group of dear people, with whom I have the freedom to come and go — as a trusted friend.

HEDDA. To the man of the house, you mean?

BRACK. Frankly, preferably primarily to the wife. And then the man. A sort of ... triangle of availability. You can't imagine how satisfying that could be all around.

HEDDA. Yes. Well. There were many, many times on this trip I just longed for some third person to talk with in those train compartments.

BRACK. All that's behind you now.

HEDDA. Oh, no. No. This is going to be a very, very long ride. We're just at the first stop along the way.

BRACK. Perhaps the thing to do is to jump off the train and stretch a little now and then.

HEDDA. I'll never get off.

BRACK. Really?

HEDDA. No. Because there's always someone at the station —

BRACK. Staring at your legs?

HEDDA. Exactly.

BRACK. But, Hedda, after all — !

HEDDA. Sorry. Not interested. I'd rather just stay on board and

33

learn everything there is to know about the medieval handicrafts of Brabant.

BRACK. All right, then, suppose a third person got on the train and joined the couple. *(Beat.)* An understanding, sympathetic friend.

HEDDA. Who is consistently entertaining.

BRACK. And not at all a specialist. Yes. Well.

HEDDA. Yes. That would be a huge relief.

TESMAN. *(From offstage.)* Oh, my ...

BRACK. The triangle is complete.

HEDDA. *(Quietly.)* And the train moves on. *(Tesman enters, loaded down with journals and books.)*

TESMAN. *(To Berta offstage.)* Oh my! Lot of work, dragging these books and journals around. I'm actually sweating, Hedda. And — Judge! You're here! Berta didn't tell me.

BRACK. I came in through the back.

HEDDA. More books? Tesman ...

TESMAN. Well. I have to keep up. Look at these journals — it's what's come out in the field while we've been gone! It's constant work!

HEDDA. In the "field"?

BRACK. Academic stuff, Hedda. Position papers. Essays. It's an industry.

HEDDA. Do you really need more journals, Tesman?

TESMAN. You can never have too many journals. I have to know what the competition is doing ... All the advances...? It's an avalanche.

HEDDA. Yes, that's probably true.

TESMAN. You have no idea. And I managed to get hold of Eilert Lovborg's new book too. Would you like to take a look, Hedda?

HEDDA. Oh, thank you. No. Maybe later.

TESMAN. I skimmed through a little of it on my way home.

BRACK. And so what do you think? From an academic specialist's point of view?

TESMAN. I think it's remarkable how much sense it makes. It's certainly unlike anything he's ever written before. I want to just drop these off in my study — and I'll just change my clothes. We don't have to leave right this minute, do we, Judge?

BRACK. Oh, no, there's no rush.

34

TESMAN. *(From offstage.)* Great, then I'll take my time. Oh, by the way, Hedda — Aunt Julia won't be coming by this evening.

HEDDA. No! Not because of that business with the hat?

TESMAN. *(Returning.)* Don't be ridiculous! Aunt Julia isn't like that! No. It's Aunt Rina. She's just not doing well at all.

HEDDA. But she's always "not doing well."

TESMAN. But it's getting much worse. Today was very bad.

HEDDA. Well, then it's natural for her to want to stay close to home. I'll have to accept that.

TESMAN. I do have to tell you how ecstatic Aunt Julia was that you'd filled out so much on our trip.

HEDDA. *(Unable to contain herself, a sudden explosion.)* Oh, Christ, it's nonstop with these aunts. *(Pause.)*

TESMAN. What?

HEDDA. Nothing.

TESMAN. Yes. All right then. *(He exits.)*

BRACK. So ... what was the "business with the hat"?

HEDDA. Oh, just — Miss Tesman had dropped her hat on that chair this morning. *(A rueful smile.)* And then I sort of pretended I thought it was the maid's.

BRACK. Hedda, why would you want to hurt that nice old lady?

HEDDA. I know. I can't help it. Something just comes over me and I can't stop myself. *(She pushes Brack's chair back into its proper place at the table.)* I can't explain it. It just happens.

BRACK. You're not really happy, is the thing.

HEDDA. Why should I be? Can you tell me exactly why I should be happy?

BRACK. For one thing, you got the house you always wanted.

HEDDA. You too? You believe that story?

BRACK. Isn't it true?

HEDDA. Here's what it is. The summer before last, Tesman used to walk me home from parties —

BRACK. I'm sorry I lived in the other direction, my dear.

HEDDA. Yes. An entirely other direction, that summer, I would say.

BRACK. Shame on you, Hedda. So. What — you and Tesman were — ?

HEDDA. One night we passed by this house. And Tesman was

35

knotted up in complete agony because he couldn't find anything to say. *(Beat.)* There was just this silence. And I felt sorry for this great thinker who —

BRACK. Did you? Really?

HEDDA. I honestly, actually did. And so, to help him out of his conversational ... quagmire — I blurted out, totally spontaneously, as an act of kindness, really just to put him out of his misery, that I'd always "loved this house and wanted to live here."

BRACK. That's it? Nothing more than that?

HEDDA. That was the extent of it. Then.

BRACK. But later...?

HEDDA. Well. Unfortunately. My frivolity had consequences, dear Judge. Didn't it?

BRACK. I have found that one's frivolity often does.

HEDDA. Thank you! So much. *(Smiling.)* So, it was my "enthusiasm" for Senator Falk's villa that brought Tesman and me together in the first place. That's it! Concluding in an engagement, and marriage, and a six-month honeymoon, et cetera, et cetera, et cetera. So there you are — you make your bed and then you've got to lie in it.

BRACK. But this is crazy — it's priceless! So you could really care less about this place, all this deluxe — ? *(He gestures, taking in the opulence.)*

HEDDA. No! God knows! Not in the least!

BRACK. Even after we made it so nice for you?

HEDDA. Nice? It smells of dead roses and dried lavender everywhere! But maybe that's Auntie Julia —

BRACK. I think that's probably a little memento mori of the late Senator's widow.

HEDDA. Yes, it is a little morbid. Isn't it? It does have sort of an air of decay. Like flowers the day after the ball. You cannot imagine how excruciatingly bored I'm going to be out here.

BRACK. Well, maybe the thing to do is — we should find something for you — sort of a goal. A plan. Some way for you to be useful.

HEDDA. And challenged at the same time ...

BRACK. Oh, naturally.

HEDDA. What would that be? — I mean — I've thought of —

36

No. It wouldn't work.

BRACK. What? Come on. Tell me.

HEDDA. If I could get Tesman to go into politics ...

BRACK. Tesman? I don't think so. He has — exactly — let's see — zero aptitude for politics!

HEDDA. No, I know that. But if I could persuade him anyway —?

BRACK. But — what satisfaction could you possibly derive from it? If there's no chance at all of him succeeding?

HEDDA. Because I'm bored! Bored! I am so bored! *(Pause.)* Look at the people who become politicians. Do you really think it's that implausible for him to end up as — say — a cabinet minister in charge of antique chairs or something — or an ambassador?

BRACK. Hedda. You know as well as I do: You have to be rich to make it in that game. Just to start off with.

HEDDA. There you have it. That's it. Isn't it? This ... cheapness, this penny-pinching little world I've ended up in. That's what makes life so ridiculous. So absolutely ludicrous. Because that's what it is.

BRACK. If you'll permit me. I think there's another problem, actually.

HEDDA. What is It?

BRACK. You've never really been stimulated by anything, have you? Truly — had a real experience?

HEDDA. Something serious, you mean? Something truly liberating?

BRACK. That's one way of putting it. But perhaps that's all about to change.

HEDDA. If what you're referring to is Tesman's struggle over his professorship — that's his problem. I will not waste a single second worrying about it.

BRACK. No, that's not — let that play itself out. But what if you're faced with a much greater ... responsibility? The biggest responsibility of them all? *(Beat.)* New duties for little Mrs. Hedda.

HEDDA. Oh, shut up! That's never going to happen — ever!

BRACK. Let's have this conversation again in about a year. At the most.

HEDDA. I have no instincts for those sorts of demands, Mr. Judge.

BRACK. Maybe you do. Perhaps they're simply submerged. And should be explored. I mean — For other women, it's the greatest joy —

HEDDA. I told you to shut up! Besides. I think I have a talent for one thing, and one thing only.

BRACK. And that is?

HEDDA. Boring myself to death. Now you know. *(Tesman is heard from offstage, ad-libbing, "What? ... I don't know.")* And speaking of which, here comes the professor.

BRACK. Now, now, now, Hedda. *(Tesman enters in evening clothes.)*

TESMAN. Hedda — have we heard from Eilert Lovborg?

HEDDA. No.

TESMAN. He's probably just going to show up then.

BRACK. You really think he'll come?

TESMAN. Yes, I do, because all of the things you told us this morning are just rumors, I'm certain of it.

BRACK. Oh. How so?

TESMAN. For one thing, Aunt Julia believes for all the world that Lovborg would never again stand in my way.

BRACK. Well then, everything is fine. We should put it out of our heads.

TESMAN. Yes, but I'd like to wait for him for as long as possible, if that's all right ...

BRACK. We have plenty of time. No one's coming to my place till seven or seven-thirty ...

TESMAN. Well, then we can keep Hedda company in the mean-time, and see what happens, right?

HEDDA. And if worst comes to worst, Mr. Lovborg can sit and talk with me.

BRACK. What do you mean, "if worst comes to worst"?

HEDDA. If he doesn't want to go with you and Tesman.

TESMAN. But Hedda, dear. Would that be appropriate? Remember — Aunt Julia isn't coming.

HEDDA. No. But Mrs. Elvsted is.

TESMAN. Oh.

HEDDA. The three of us will drink a cup of tea together.

TESMAN. In that case it's fine.

BRACK. And it might be the best thing for him.

HEDDA. Why?

BRACK. Mrs. Tesman, haven't you always said that my bachelor drinking parties are fit only for men of the highest moral character?

HEDDA. Well, surely Mr. Lovborg, being such a reformed sinner, now falls right into that category…?

BERTA. *(Entering.)* Ma'am. There's a gentleman here for you.

HEDDA. Good. Show him in.

TESMAN. It's got to be him. Amazing. Simply amazing. *(Berta shows Eilert Lovborg into the room. He is the same age as Tesman, but looks more worn, despite the elegant new suit he wears. She closes the door behind him. Crossing to greet him.)* My dear Eilert — at last — we meet again.

LOVBORG. Thank you for your letter, George. *(Approaching Hedda.)* May I shake hands with you, too, Mrs. Tesman?

HEDDA. *(Taking his hand.)* We're so happy to see you, Mr. Lovborg. *(Indicating Judge Brack.)* I'm not sure if you two — ?

LOVBORG. *(Crossing to the Judge.)* Judge Brack, I believe.

BRACK. It's been a very long time.

TESMAN. Please, Eilert, make yourself at home — right, Hedda? Is it true that you're really thinking of moving back to town?

LOVBORG. That's my plan, yes.

TESMAN. Well, it makes sense — listen — you — I've just gotten hold of your new book, but I haven't had a second to read it properly yet.

LOVBORG. Save yourself the trouble.

TESMAN. Good Lord! What do you mean?

LOVBORG. There isn't very much to it.

TESMAN. Come on, now.

BRACK. But it's getting such attention.

LOVBORG. Yes, that was exactly what I wanted. I wrote a book that's pitched precisely to the general public. No one could possibly disagree with it.

BRACK. Very clever of you. You pulled it off, apparently.

TESMAN. Yes, but, why would you …

LOVBORG. Because what I would like is to somehow try to build up a position for myself. If it's even possible at this stage. And start over.

TESMAN. Yes. That's — of course — I would think you would — right.

LOVBORG. *(Holding up the thick manuscript he's been carrying.)* But when this one comes out — George Tesman — I'd love for you to read it. Because this is the one. The real thing. I put my whole self into this book.

TESMAN. Really? What sort of book is it?

LOVBORG. The sequel.

TESMAN. To what?

LOVBORG. To the book.

TESMAN. The one just out?

LOVBORG. Of course.

TESMAN. But Eilert — that one comes right up to the present.

LOVBORG. Right. And this one deals with the future.

TESMAN. The future? But we don't know anything about that!

LOVBORG. True. But there are things worth saying about it anyway. Take a look. It's in two parts.

TESMAN. That's not your handwriting.

LOVBORG. I dictated it. The first deals with how the various systems at work on our society are changing. And — the second part is sort of ... an analysis of where those changes might take us, and a projection of how it might end up.

TESMAN. How amazing! Extraordinary. It would never have occurred to me to even attempt anything like that.

HEDDA. *(To Judge Brack.)* Hmn ... true. It wouldn't.

LOVBORG. Well. I brought it because I was hoping to share a little bit of it with you this evening.

TESMAN. Oh, Eilert. That's so generous of you — but tonight? *(Glances over at Judge Brack.)* Tonight it's not really good.

LOVBORG. Another time then. There's no hurry.

BRACK. I should explain, Mr. Lovborg. There's a little party at my place this evening — mostly in honor of Tesman.

LOVBORG. Oh, well, in that case, I won't —

BRACK. And I would be very pleased if you would join us.

LOVBORG. *(Wrapping up his manuscript.)* No. I can't. Thank you, though.

BRACK. Oh, come on! It's just a small select group, and it's sure to be "lively" as Hedda — as Mrs. Tesman would say.

LOVBORG. Yes. I don't doubt it, but nevertheless —
BRACK. You could bring your manuscript and read it to Tesman in my study.
TESMAN. Why not, Eilert! You can do that, can't you?
HEDDA. But my dear, what if Mr. Lovborg just doesn't want to? I'm sure he'd much rather stay put and just have supper with me.
LOVBORG. With you, Mrs. Tesman?
HEDDA. And Mrs. Elvsted.
LOVBORG. Ah. *(Casually.)* I ran into her briefly this afternoon.
HEDDA. Oh, did you? Well, she's coming over! And so that means you really have very little choice, because otherwise there'll be no one to see her home. She'll be stranded here like a little bird.
LOVBORG. Right. That's true. Yes. Thank you, Mrs. Tesman. In that case, I suppose I have to stay.
HEDDA. Let me just tell the maid. *(Hedda crosses up to the library and rings the bell. Berta appears. Hedda talks with her.)*
TESMAN. So, Eilert, uhm. Is it this new subject — the future — is that what you'll be lecturing about?
LOVBORG. Yes.
TESMAN. Because I heard at the bookstore that you're going to be giving a series of talks this fall.
LOVBORG. I hope that doesn't bother you, Tesman...?
TESMAN. Why, God no! No! Why would it? No. But — ?
LOVBORG. I can certainly understand that I might be getting in your way.
TESMAN. I could hardly expect that for my sake, you'd —
LOVBORG. I'll wait until you've been given your appointment.
TESMAN. You'll wait? You — you don't — but don't you intend to compete for it?
LOVBORG. With you? No. I will not compete with you for a job, Tesman. *(Beat.)* No. I only want to win over you. To be more respected, and more admired than you. *(Beat.)* In the eyes of the world.
TESMAN. My God, Aunt Julia was right! I knew it! Hedda — did you hear that? Eilert has no intention of standing in our way!
HEDDA. *Our* way? Leave me out of it. *(She crosses up to the library to oversee Berta's preparations for serving punch.)*
TESMAN. But what about you, Judge — what do you have to

41

say about all this?

BRACK. *(Carefully.)* I think that honor and victory can be wonderful things —

TESMAN. Right, yes, but still —

HEDDA. *(Returning to the main room.)* Huh. You look like you've just been hit by lightning.

TESMAN. Yes — just about — that's what it feels —

BRACK. That's because a thunderstorm just passed over us, Mrs. Tesman.

HEDDA. Wouldn't you gentlemen like a nice glass of rum punch? Berta has a way of making it ... just so.

BRACK. One for the road? Tesman?

TESMAN. Great idea, Hedda! With ... this weight off my mind! Sure ... *(Tesman exits into the library. Judge Brack follows.)*

HEDDA. Please, Mr. Lovborg. You too.

LOVBORG. No. Thank you. Not for me.

BRACK. *(Pausing on his exit.)* Good God, Mr. Lovborg — a little punch isn't exactly poison.

LOVBORG. Perhaps not for everyone.

HEDDA. I'll keep Mr. Lovborg company in the meantime.

TESMAN. *(From offstage, in the library.)* All right, Hedda, dear, you do that. *(Judge Brack follows Tesman into the library.)*

HEDDA. *(She watches them leave, then crosses to the desk and picks up the photo album.)* Would you like to see some photographs of our trip? We got a camera! Tesman and I came home through the Tyrol. It's very dramatic. *(Lovborg just stares at her. She turns the pages and moves closer to him. Judge Brack is watching them, and Hedda knows this. She speaks carefully.)* Do you see this mountain here, Mr. Lovborg? The Ortler Alps. Tesman's labeled all of them. Meticulously. As you can see. Here it is: "The Ortler Alps near Meran."

LOVBORG. *(Quietly.)* Hedda Gabler.

HEDDA. Shh!

LOVBORG. Hedda Gabler.

HEDDA. Yes. That used to be my name. When we first knew each other.

LOVBORG. And now I have to learn how not to call you Hedda Gabler ...

HEDDA. Well. Start practicing. The sooner you get used to it, the better. *(Laughter from the gentlemen in the library.)*

LOVBORG. Hedda Gabler, married? And to George Tesman?

HEDDA. So it goes.

LOVBORG. Oh, Hedda, Hedda — how could you throw yourself away like that?

HEDDA. *(An urgent command.)* All right. Enough. This isn't the time for this. *(She steals a glance toward the library.)*

LOVBORG. What do you mean?

TESMAN. *(From library.)* Hedda ...

HEDDA. *(Setting the photo album down on the table, open.)* And this one, Mr. Lovborg, is the view from the Ampezzo Valley.

TESMAN. *(Entering from the library, smoking a cigarette.)* I just wanted to ask if we should bring in a little punch. For you, at least.

HEDDA. Yes, thank you. And some biscuits, perhaps.

TESMAN. Cigarette?

HEDDA. No.

TESMAN. Right. *(He returns to the library.)*

LOVBORG. Answer me, Hedda ... Hedda, how could you do such a thing?

HEDDA. If you keep on saying "Hedda, Hedda, Hedda," I won't talk to you at all.

LOVBORG. Can't I say your name even when we're alone?

HEDDA. No. You can think it. But you can't say it.

LOVBORG. Ah! I understand. It demeans your love for George Tesman.

HEDDA. Love? Don't be absurd.

LOVBORG. Then you don't love him?

HEDDA. Nor will I be unfaithful to him. I'm not going down that road.

LOVBORG. Well, then, you didn't ...

HEDDA. Shh! *(Tesman reenters from the library with a tray of punch and biscuits.)*

TESMAN. Here we go. Goodies. *(He sets the tray down on the center table.)*

HEDDA. George, why are you serving us?

TESMAN. *(Pouring out the glasses of punch.)* Because giving you pleasure makes me so incredibly happy.

HEDDA. You've filled two glasses. Mr. Lovborg doesn't want any.

TESMAN. Yes, but Mrs. Elvsted will be here soon.

HEDDA. Right. Mrs. Elvsted.

TESMAN. Had you forgotten her?

HEDDA. We've been so engrossed in these. *(Shows him the pictures.)* Remember this little village?

TESMAN. Oh, isn't that right below the Brenner Pass? Where we stayed one night...?

HEDDA. Yes, and met all those lively summer people.

TESMAN. *(Striking the serving tray and returning to the library.)* Yes. You'd have loved it there, Eilert. *(He exits.)*

LOVBORG. Answer one thing, Hedda.

HEDDA. Yes?

LOVBORG. You didn't love me, either? Was there nothing there at all?

HEDDA. Well. I wonder. I don't know. Because it seems to me that we were very close comrades — two good friends — You were so unguarded with me. You shared everything. You had no defenses.

LOVBORG. Isn't that what you wanted?

HEDDA. When I look back on it now, there was something thrilling and dangerous about it all. The secret aspect. *(Beat.)* A friendship that no one had any idea about.

LOVBORG. I'd come over to your father's in the afternoons — and the General would sit by the window, reading the papers, his back turned to us —

HEDDA. And we'd sit there, in the corner — on the sofa —

LOVBORG. Always with the same magazine in front of us —

HEDDA. Yes. For lack of a picture album.

LOVBORG. And me pouring my heart out to you, confessing things about myself that nobody else knew! About how I'd go out drinking, insane, degrading myself in any way I could, day after day, for weeks at a time — *(Beat.)* What was it, Hedda, that made me tell you so much...?

HEDDA. Do you think I had some sort of power over you?

LOVBORG. Yes! What other explanation is there? Your sly questions...?

HEDDA. All I did was ask you questions. You answered freely.

LOVBORG. Yes. Because you asked without any shame at all!

HEDDA. Well, you seemed extremely willing to answer anything, so ...

LOVBORG. That's exactly what I don't understand — now — looking back. *(Laughter is heard from the gentlemen offstage.)* Hedda. Wasn't there love at the core of it? *(Beat.)* I mean — When I came to you with all my lurid, grotesque confessions? Didn't you want to absolve me? Purify me? Save me?

HEDDA. No. Not quite.

LOVBORG. Why, then?

HEDDA. A young girl — you find it so hard to accept that a young girl might —

LOVBORG. What?

HEDDA. Want — just a little peek in at a world which — Which she is not permitted to know anything about at all. Nothing!

LOVBORG. So that was it?

HEDDA. Part of it. I think. Yes. In part.

LOVBORG. So. All you wanted was information? *(Judge Brack begins to play the piano in the library.)* Huh. So. If that was the case, why couldn't it keep going?

HEDDA. Oh. That's your fault.

LOVBORG. You broke it off.

HEDDA. Because of what was happening. When it was on the verge of becoming dangerous. When — you were at the point of taking advantage of me — shameful! — After I trusted you so much ...

LOVBORG. Then why didn't you shoot me! You threatened to! Why didn't you just do it?

HEDDA. Because I was too afraid of scandal. *("Scandal" is loud enough to catch Tesman's ear upstage. He looks to Hedda, then back to Brack at the piano.)*

LOVBORG. Yes, Hedda. That's right. Exactly. Deep down you are a coward.

HEDDA. A total coward. But lucky for you, as it turns out. Now that you've been so nicely regenerated at the Elvsteds.

LOVBORG. I know what Thea has told you.

HEDDA. And have you reciprocated by telling her about us?

LOVBORG. Not a word. She's too stupid to understand.

45

HEDDA. Stupid?

LOVBORG. When it comes to that sort of thing, she's stupid.

HEDDA. Yes. So she's stupid. And I'm a coward. Well. There is *something* I can confess. The night I was too scared to shoot you — ?

LOVBORG. Yes?

HEDDA. That wasn't the most cowardly thing I did that night.

LOVBORG. Oh, Hedda — ! God! I see it now — You were like me — starving for life.

HEDDA. Careful! There's no point in thinking that way. *(Berta enters with Mrs. Elvsted. Tesman crosses into the room to greet her.)* Thea! Darling — finally! Please come in.

MRS. ELVSTED. Maybe I should spend a moment with your husband...?

HEDDA. Don't be silly! Let them be. They're about to leave anyway.

MRS. ELVSTED. They're leaving?

HEDDA. Yes. For an evening of wild drunken male revelry. Exciting, isn't it?

MRS. ELVSTED. *(To Lovborg.)* You're not going, are you?

LOVBORG. No.

HEDDA. Mr. Lovborg — is staying here with us.

MRS. ELVSTED. Oh, it's good to be here!

LOVBORG. *(Helping Mrs. Elvsted into a chair at the center table.)* Isn't she lovely to look at?

HEDDA. Only to look at?

LOVBORG. Yes. Because she and I are true comrades. We believe in, trust one another. And can say anything to each other.

HEDDA. Never anything sly, Mr. Lovborg?

MRS. ELVSTED. He says that I've inspired him!

HEDDA. Really? He said that?

LOVBORG. And she, Mrs. Tesman, has the courage of her convictions.

MRS. ELVSTED. God! No — Me? Courage!

LOVBORG. Enormous courage. When it comes to me.

HEDDA. Yes. Courage. Ah! If one only had that ...

LOVBORG. Then what?

HEDDA. One could perhaps actually live. But Thea — come

now — have a nice cold glass of punch.

MRS. ELVSTED. No thanks. I never drink.

HEDDA. Well, then you, Mr. Lovborg?

LOVBORG. No. Thank you. Nor me.

MRS. ELVSTED. No! He doesn't either!

HEDDA. But if I wanted you to?

LOVBORG. It makes no difference.

HEDDA. Poor me! Am I powerless over you?

LOVBORG. In this particular area, yes.

HEDDA. Seriously, Mr. Lovborg. I do think you should have a little tiny wee drink, just for your own sake.

MRS. ELVSTED. Hedda!

LOVBORG. And why is that?

HEDDA. Or rather, for other people's sake.

LOVBORG. Ah. Uh-huh.

HEDDA. Otherwise people will think that deep down you don't trust yourself. And are really actually afraid.

MRS. ELVSTED. Hedda, don't.

LOVBORG. People can think whatever they like. I couldn't care less.

MRS. ELVSTED. Yes! That's right.

HEDDA. I saw it *so* clearly in Judge Brack just now.

LOVBORG. What did you see?

HEDDA. That goatish little smile on his lips, and he glanced over at Tesman pityingly when you wouldn't dare go to their gruesome little soiree.

LOVBORG. What do you mean, "wouldn't dare"?

HEDDA. Well, isn't that how Judge Brack obviously understood it?

LOVBORG. Fine. Let him.

HEDDA. So you're really not going?

LOVBORG. I'm staying here with you and Thea.

MRS. ELVSTED. That's right, Hedda. See?

HEDDA. *(Crossing to Thea.)* Yes. I do. Strong as a rock. An unshakable will. True to your word. Exactly how a man should be. Isn't that what I told you when you came to us this morning, so hysterically?

LOVBORG. Hysterically?

MRS. ELVSTED. Hedda —

HEDDA. Well, I mean — look at him. See? There's absolutely no need to live in terror that he's going to — Right. So now let's cheer up and enjoy ourselves!

MRS. ELVSTED. Oh, God ...

LOVBORG. What is this?

MRS. ELVSTED. Hedda! What are you saying?

HEDDA. Quiet. That disgusting Judge keeps looking at us.

LOVBORG. *(Turning to Mrs. Elvsted, furious.)* To "live in terror"? For my sake?

MRS. ELVSTED. Hedda ... why?

LOVBORG. *(Fixated on her.)* And ... was that the extent of your trust in me? "Living in terror ..."?

MRS. ELVSTED. Please, darling, listen to me —

LOVBORG. *(Raising a punch glass.)* Your health, Thea. *(He drinks.)*

MRS. ELVSTED. Oh, Hedda. How could you do this?

HEDDA. Me? Are you out of your mind?

LOVBORG. And a toast to you, Mrs. Tesman. Thanks for the truth. Long live the truth. *(He drains the glass and sets it on the table.)*

HEDDA. All right. That's enough for now. Remember. You're going to a party.

MRS. ELVSTED. No!

HEDDA. Shh! They're watching you.

LOVBORG. Thea. Tell me something. Honestly — Did you have an agreement? You and he? That you would follow me to town and watch over me? Or — or did the commissioner have the idea — because, after all, he must need me in his office, or maybe he just missed me at the poker table? Is that it?

MRS. ELVSTED. Eilert. Please. Eilert.

LOVBORG. *(Picking up the second glass.)* A toast to the commissioner too! *(He drains the second glass.)*

HEDDA. *(Crossing toward him and taking the glass away.)* Enough. Remember you're going to Judge Brack's and giving a little reading for Tesman.

LOVBORG. *(Taking the glass back from her and setting it on the table.)* I shouldn't have done this. *(Beat.)* Stupid of me. *(Beat.)* To react like that. I'm sorry, Thea. But you'll see — you and everyone.

I may have fallen once, but I've stood up again. Haven't I? And only because of you ...

MRS. ELVSTED. Thank God. *(Brack and Tesman have reentered, ready to head out.)*

BRACK. Well, Mrs. Tesman — our time here is up.

HEDDA. Yes, I suppose it is.

LOVBORG. *(Picking up his manuscript.)* Mine too, Judge.

MRS. ELVSTED. Oh, Eilert. Don't.

LOVBORG. You were kind enough to invite me to come along.

BRACK. Oh, you'll come?

LOVBORG. Yes. If I may.

BRACK. I'm delighted.

LOVBORG. *(To Tesman.)* I'd like to show you a few parts before I send it in to the publisher.

TESMAN. How wonderful! But, Hedda dear, how will Mrs. Elvsted get home?

HEDDA. Oh, we'll figure that out.

LOVBORG. I'll come by and pick her up. Around ... ten. Is that all right?

HEDDA. Perfect.

TESMAN. Well, then everything is settled. But you mustn't expect me that early, Hedda.

HEDDA. Darling. You stay out as long as you like.

MRS. ELVSTED. Mr. Lovborg. I'll be waiting for you.

LOVBORG. Yes. I understand.

BRACK. And now, gentlemen, the pleasure car is leaving! And I'm sure it's going to be a "lively" trip, as a certain lovely lady would say.

HEDDA. Oh, and if only that lovely lady could be there, an invisible witness.

BRACK. Why invisible?

HEDDA. If for no other reason than to hear some of your uncensored, unbridled wit.

BRACK. Oh-ho! No, no, no! I would advise the lovely lady against trying it.

TESMAN. Hedda, you really are something. Can you imagine! Eh? I mean — !

BRACK. Well. Good night, ladies.

LOVBORG. See you at ten, then. *(The men exit. Berta enters from the library with a lit lamp and sets it on the center table. She exits to the library.)*
MRS. ELVSTED. Hedda! What's going to happen?
HEDDA. I'll tell you exactly what's going to happen. He'll be back here at ten o'clock. I can see him now. With vine leaves in his hair. Glorious and proud and glowing.
MRS. ELVSTED. If only I could believe that.
HEDDA. And then — you'll see — he'll have finally reclaimed himself completely! And will always be free!
MRS. ELVSTED. I hope you're right.
HEDDA. I'm telling you. That's how he'll come back. It's a test, which he will pass. You see — you can doubt. But I believe in him. And now we'll see —
MRS. ELVSTED. What are you trying to do, Hedda?
HEDDA. For once in my life, I would like to have some power over someone's destiny.
MRS. ELVSTED. You don't have that?
HEDDA. I don't. And I never have. Oh, if you had any idea how poor I am. And you're allowed to be so rich! So rich! *(She embraces Mrs. Elvsted, then releases her. She crosses to the center table, picks up the lit lamp, crosses back to Mrs. Elvsted and grabs her by the hair.)* You know, I think I'll burn your hair off after all.
MRS. ELVSTED. *(Struggling to get away from Hedda.)* Let go of me! Let go of me! You scare me, Hedda! *(Berta enters from the library.)*
BERTA. There's tea waiting in the dining room, ma'am.
HEDDA. Good, good. We're coming. *(Berta exits.)*
MRS. ELVSTED. *(Heading for the hallway door.)* No, no, no! I'd rather go home — now! Right this second!
HEDDA. *(Crossing to her.)* Nonsense! *(Leading Mrs. Elvsted toward the library.)* First you're going to have some tea, you foolish little girl, and then, my dear, at ten o'clock, Eilert Lovborg will be back! With vine leaves in his hair. *(They exit into the library.)*

# ACT THREE

*Hedda is asleep on the chaise. Mrs. Elvsted is asleep on a chair by the stove. Berta enters from the library with a coffee service on a tray. She sets the tray on the center table. The doorbell rings offstage left. Berta exits to the hallway. The noise wakes Mrs. Elvsted.*

MRS. ELVSTED.  Oh God, they're *still* not back! *(Berta returns with a letter.)* Yes? Has someone come?
BERTA.  Yes. A girl came by with this letter.
MRS. ELVSTED.  A letter! Give it to me!
BERTA.  No, it's for the doctor, ma'am.
MRS. ELVSTED.  Oh.
BERTA.  Miss Tesman's maid brought it. I'll leave it here on the table.
MRS. ELVSTED.  Yes, do.
BERTA.  Do you mind if I take the lamp out?
MRS. ELVSTED.  Yes. Take it out. It'll be dawn soon, anyway.
BERTA.  *(Picking up the lamp.)* It's already daylight, ma'am.
MRS. ELVSTED.  It's daylight — ! And they're still not home!
BERTA.  It's what I thought would happen.
MRS. ELVSTED.  You did?
BERTA.  Yes, of course — when I heard that a certain gentleman was back in town, running around with them, yes! Because we've heard a great deal about this gentleman over the years.
MRS. ELVSTED.  Don't talk so loudly. You'll wake up Mrs. Tesman.
BERTA.  Oh my. Yes. Let's let her sleep, poor thing. Should I put a little more wood on the fire?
MRS. ELVSTED.  Thanks, not for my sake.
BERTA.  All right. *(She exits into the library, closing the doors behind her.)*

HEDDA. What was that?

MRS. ELVSTED. It was just the maid —

HEDDA. In here — ? Oh. Yes. Now I remember. What time is it, Thea?

MRS. ELVSTED. It's just after six.

HEDDA. What time did Tesman come in?

MRS. ELVSTED. He didn't.

HEDDA. He's not back?

MRS. ELVSTED. No one is.

HEDDA. And we sat here and waited up till four o'clock — !

MRS. ELVSTED. Just waiting and waiting —

HEDDA. We really shouldn't have bothered.

MRS. ELVSTED. You were actually able to sleep...?

HEDDA. Yes, fine, no problem. Why? Didn't you?

MRS. ELVSTED. No, not at all, Hedda! It was impossible.

HEDDA. Now there. It's all fine. You can guess what happened.

MRS. ELVSTED. What? Tell me!

HEDDA. Clearly, their party went on all night.

MRS. ELVSTED. Oh, God yes. But still —

HEDDA. And I assume that Tesman didn't want to stumble in drunk, in the middle of the night. Afraid he'd be caught.

MRS. ELVSTED. But then where would he go?

HEDDA. To his Aunties', of course. After all — they do keep his old room ready and waiting for him. Fresh sheets and flowers.

MRS. ELVSTED. No. He can't be there. He just got a letter from them. It's right here.

HEDDA. Huh. That's Aunt Julia's handwriting all right. Well, then he must've stayed at the Judge's. *(Beat.)* And Eilert Lovborg is sitting there, with vine leaves in his hair. Still reading to them.

MRS. ELVSTED. You're just talking. You don't believe a word you're saying.

HEDDA. Thea. Do you know what a fool you are? Do you?

MRS. ELVSTED. I know. I am. It's true.

HEDDA. And I have to tell you. You look dead tired.

MRS. ELVSTED. I feel dead tired.

HEDDA. Well then, listen to me. Here's what you do. Go into my room and stretch out on the bed for a little while.

MRS. ELVSTED. No. I couldn't sleep.

HEDDA. Yes you will.

MRS. ELVSTED. But your husband's sure to come in and I want to know right away —

HEDDA. I'll tell you the moment — the instant — he comes in.

MRS. ELVSTED. Yes? Oh — do you promise, Hedda?

HEDDA. You can count on it. Just go and get some sleep. *(Hedda takes Mrs. Elvsted to the library doors and opens them for her exit.)*

MRS. ELVSTED. Thanks. I'll try. *(She exits into the library toward the stage left hallway. Hedda rings the bell for Berta, crosses back down to the chaise and picks up the blanket to wrap up in it. She then crosses to the window and opens the drapes. Berta enters from the library.)*

BERTA. Is there anything ma'am needs?

HEDDA. Yes. Would you put more wood on the fire? It's freezing in here.

BERTA. Why, my God, of course! We'll warm it up right away. *(She crosses to the stove and places two logs on the fire. Berta then returns the chair that Mrs. Elvsted was sitting in to the center table and adjusts the ottoman to its place in front of the stove. While this is going on, Hedda crosses to the desk, opens a drawer and pulls out a hand mirror. She makes a few adjustments to her hair and replaces the mirror in the desk drawer. Hedda looks at Berta to leave and Berta hurries into the library and offstage. Hedda then replaces the blanket on the chaise and crosses to the stove. She sits on the ottoman and places a few more logs on the fire. As she does this, Tesman enters with his jacket folded up in his arms.)*

HEDDA. Good morning.

TESMAN. Hedda! But what on earth are you doing up so early?

HEDDA. Yes, I'm up very early today.

TESMAN. I was sure you'd still be sleeping — You're up? Imagine!

HEDDA. Not so loud. Mrs. Elvsted's trying to get some sleep in my room.

TESMAN. She was here all night?

HEDDA. Well. Considering. No one came to pick her up.

TESMAN. Right.

HEDDA. So was it just a cornucopia of fun at the Judge's?

TESMAN. Were you worried about me? Eh? Is that it? Hedda?

HEDDA. No. Not remotely. All I asked was, "Did you enjoy

yourself?"

TESMAN. Oh, yes, in the early part of the evening, when Eilert read me a bit of his book. We were there so early! Brack had to get ready — so Eilert read to me.

HEDDA. Tell me.

TESMAN. It's — I have to say — an amazing piece of work. Utterly unique. And I think one of the most original things ever written. Certainly on the subject of —

HEDDA. No, I didn't mean the book —

TESMAN. Yes — but I have to admit one thing to you, Hedda. When he was finished reading, I was overwhelmed with a kind of ugly feeling.

HEDDA. Ugly?

TESMAN. I — I — I ... found myself envious of Eilert. Awful. Covetous. *(Beat.)* That he had written this amazing thing. That it was a towering achievement. And I was jealous. Can you imagine, Hedda?

HEDDA. Oh, yes. I think I can.

TESMAN. And — and — to know — that this man — with all his prodigious gifts is still lost. Still — completely unsalvageable.

HEDDA. You mean — what — ? That he has an appetite for life? That he's more courageous than most people?

TESMAN. No — ! Good Lord, no — ! I mean there's nothing moderate about him. He has no way of stopping himself, you see.

HEDDA. What happened?

TESMAN. The evening became a bacchanal, I would say, Hedda. Eilert made a long, rambling speech about the woman who "inspired his work." His phrase.

HEDDA. Did he say who it was?

TESMAN. No. But it has to be Mrs. Elvsted. Doesn't it?

HEDDA. Uh-huh.

TESMAN. Imagine that.

HEDDA. So — where did you leave him?

TESMAN. On the way here, the party finally broke up. Brack was walking with us. He needed some air. We all did. And we wanted to make sure Eilert got home, because he was so smashed, absolutely blind drunk, you know.

HEDDA. Right. I can picture it.

TESMAN. But then the most amazing thing happened. Or maybe I should say the most distressing thing. Oh, God. I almost hate talking about it, if only for Eilert's sake —

HEDDA. Go on, Tesman.

TESMAN. We're walking into town. And I sort of lagged behind to ... to ... for a moment. Just for a second ...

HEDDA. Yes, yes, good God, what?

TESMAN. So I run to catch up with them — and what do you think I find on the side of the road...?

HEDDA. I have no idea.

TESMAN. Please, please, promise me you won't say a word to anyone about this. For Eilert's sake. *(He unfolds his jacket and removes the manuscript.)* Can you believe it? I found this.

HEDDA. Isn't that what he had with him?

TESMAN. Yes! Exactly! His manuscript! The whole precious, irreplaceable thing! And he lost it! Without even noticing! Can you imagine, Hedda? It's heartbreaking!

HEDDA. But why didn't you give it back to him right away?

TESMAN. In his condition? I didn't dare.

HEDDA. And you didn't tell anyone else you'd found it?

TESMAN. Of course not. I'd never do that. For Eilert's sake.

HEDDA. Then there's no one who knows you have it.

TESMAN. No. And nobody can know.

HEDDA. You never told Lovborg you found it?

TESMAN. I didn't have a chance. As soon as we came into town, he and a couple of the others disappeared.

HEDDA. Maybe they got him home.

TESMAN. Probably. And Brack ended up going back home ...

HEDDA. So then where did your revelries end?

TESMAN. Oh, a bunch of us ended up at one of their places, having morning coffee — *(Beat.)* Anyway. The point is, as soon as I've rested a little and poor Eilert has slept it off, I'll take it to him.

HEDDA. *(Reaching for the manuscript.)* No. Not right away. Let me read it first.

TESMAN. *(Holding on to the manuscript.)* Hedda, my darling. I wouldn't dare do that!

HEDDA. You wouldn't ... dare?

TESMAN. Good God, no. Because when he realizes what he's

done, he'll go out of his mind with anxiety. He'll go absolutely insane! He told me that he doesn't even have a copy. *(Hedda releases the manuscript and steps back.)* Can you imagine? Not a single copy! This is it.

HEDDA. Wouldn't he be able to rewrite it? I mean — from scratch?

TESMAN. I just honestly don't know how you would do that. No. It wouldn't be the same. Because the inspiration — you can feel the way it's all written in sort of a rush, Hedda. At the moment of inspiration …

HEDDA. Right. Yes. That's it, isn't it…? *(Beat.)* Oh, there's a letter for you. *(She picks up the letter and turns to Tesman.)*

TESMAN. No. Really? *(He leaves the manuscript on the chaise, rises and takes the letter from Hedda.)*

HEDDA. It came early this morning.

TESMAN. *(Opens the letter.)* It's Aunt Julia. Oh, Hedda! She says Aunt Rina's dying.

HEDDA. Well. That's — we've been expecting that.

TESMAN. *(Rushing to gather his things.)* And if I want to see her one last time, I've got to hurry. I've got to race right over there.

HEDDA. Race?

TESMAN. Oh, Hedda, darling, is there any way I could get you to come with me?

HEDDA. No, no. Please. Don't ask me that. I can't be around death or illness now. I just can't.

TESMAN. Yes, of course. I understand. I hope I'm not too late, Hedda — !

HEDDA. Well, if you just race along …

BERTA. *(Entering from the stage left hallway.)* Judge Brack's here, asking if he may come in.

TESMAN. Oh, God. I can't see him right now!

HEDDA. But I can. Send him in. *(Berta exits.)* The manuscript, Tesman! *(She picks it up.)*

TESMAN. Yes, give it to me!

HEDDA. No, I'll keep it till you get back. *(She takes the manuscript upstage and into the library. Judge Brack enters from stage left and Berta closes the door behind him.)* Well, you're certainly the early bird, Judge.

BRACK. Yes, extraordinary how that works, isn't it? *(To Tesman.)* So — you're already up and running?

TESMAN. Yes. It's Auntie Rina; I think it's almost over for her, poor thing. I can't believe it. I've got to get over there.

BRACK. Oh God. Really? Then don't let me hold you up, at a time like this ...

TESMAN. *(Shaking Judge Brack's hand as he exits.)* Yes, I'm sorry. I've got to run. Goodbye! *(Tesman exits.)*

HEDDA. So you boys apparently had a big night, didn't you?

BRACK. I haven't even had a chance to change my clothes, Hedda.

HEDDA. You too, huh?

BRACK. So what did Tesman say about our wild party?

HEDDA. Just some boring details that end up at what sounds suspiciously like a coffee klatch.

BRACK. Yes. I heard about the coffee. But Lovborg wasn't with them by then.

HEDDA. No. They took him home first.

BRACK. Tesman?

HEDDA. No. He said some of the others did.

BRACK. George Tesman really is a simple soul, isn't he, Hedda?

HEDDA. God knows. But — Judge. Are you keeping something from me?

BRACK. That, I'm sorry to say, is a reasonable conclusion.

HEDDA. All right then. Let's hear. *(She sits.)* Go ahead. I'm waiting. You've got my full attention, Your Honor.

BRACK. I had a particular reason for keeping an eye on certain of my guests last night.

HEDDA. Really? You did? That's so unlike you. And was Eilert Lovborg perhaps amongst them?

BRACK. In all candor, yes. He was.

HEDDA. Well, now I'm really curious.

BRACK. Do you know where he and a couple of the other gentlemen ended up?

HEDDA. If you don't think it's too shocking to tell me, go ahead.

BRACK. Oh, I think you can hear it. They ended up at an exceptionally vivid little debauch.

HEDDA. I see. As debauches go, of course. It was lively?

BRACK. The liveliest.

HEDDA. Go on.

BRACK. Lovborg and the others had been invited earlier. Which I knew. But Lovborg had very politely declined, in the spirit of his newly found reformation.

HEDDA. But he ended up going anyway?

BRACK. Well, what can one say? The spirit just moved him at my party. And the flesh was weak ...

HEDDA. Yes. I hear he was quite inspired ...

BRACK. Violently inspired. His mind turned to all that he was missing. You know, the thing about men is our principles can be a little bit tenuous, under pressure.

HEDDA. Yes, but I'm sure you're the exception, aren't you, Judge? But what happened with Lovborg?

BRACK. The last stop on his little trip? He ended up at a certain "Madame Diana's."

HEDDA. "Madame Diana"?

BRACK. It was Madame Diana who was having the soiree. For a very select group of men and women.

HEDDA. Tell me: Is she a redhead?

BRACK. That's the one.

HEDDA. Sort of a ... singer?

BRACK. I believe she has many talents. Not least amongst them: voracious hunter of men. It sounds like you've heard of her. Lovborg was one of her favorites. When he still had promise.

HEDDA. And so how did it all end?

BRACK. Not well, I'm afraid. She went from hugs and kisses to kicking and punching fairly quickly.

HEDDA. Directed at Lovborg?

BRACK. Exactly. He accused her of having stolen his journal. In any case, he apparently went right over the edge.

HEDDA. Concluding in...?

BRACK. Oh, well. You know. These things. How could it end? A fairly impressive free-for-all, complete with the arrival of the police.

HEDDA. Right. Of course. The police.

BRACK. Yes, and it's going to end up being one of Mr. Lovborg's more costly exploits. A staggeringly foolish, blindly reckless man,

I've got to say.

HEDDA. Yes?

BRACK. He resisted arrest, started swinging, hit a policeman in the eye, ripped one of their uniforms. They took him to the station.

HEDDA. And ... how do you know all this?

BRACK. From the police.

HEDDA. So that's how it went. No vine leaves in his hair ...

BRACK. Vine leaves, Hedda? What're you talking about?

HEDDA. Nothing. But tell me this, Judge. What made you so very intent on keeping track of Lovborg?

BRACK. In the first place, I can't be completely indifferent to the fact that it's going to be revealed in court that he came right from my house —

HEDDA. In court? It's going to go to court?

BRACK. Yes, it's set in motion. No stopping it. And as a friend of the family, don't you think I owe you and Tesman at the very least a full account of his nocturnal exploits?

HEDDA. Well, why exactly?

BRACK. Because I strongly suspect he'll try and use you as a cover.

HEDDA. What makes you think that?

BRACK. Come now, Hedda. We're not blind. Do you think this Mrs. Elvsted is going to quietly drift back up to the country? To the commissioner?

HEDDA. Yes, but — even assuming there was something between them, there are lots of other places they could meet.

BRACK. Oh, no. Not one single home. From now on there'll be no respectable house open to them. Every door will be closed.

HEDDA. And you think mine should be too? Is that what you're saying?

BRACK. Yes! I have to say, yes, sorry. I would find it extremely agitating were this man to have free rein here! If he came on as some sort of interloper! Forcing his way into —

HEDDA. The triangle?

BRACK. Precisely. I would feel almost as if I'd been turned out of my own home.

HEDDA. I see. So you really do need to be top dog, is that what you're saying?

BRACK. Yes. That, I think, is the point ... *(Beat.)* And it is a point which I intend to achieve with any and every means at my disposal.

HEDDA. Hmn. Judge. You are ... *(Beat.)* ... A dangerous man, aren't you? When cornered?

BRACK. Do you think? Am I? Oh.

HEDDA. Yes. I'm beginning to. Which is fine, as long as you don't have any kind of power over me.

BRACK. Yes, that's probably true. If I did — who knows what I might do? I could be capable of anything ...

HEDDA. That sounds just a little like a threat, Your Honor?

BRACK. No, God no. Not at all! I'm merely saying that a triangle has to be fortified and defended. Voluntarily.

HEDDA. I agree.

BRACK. Well, I've said all I have to say. I'd better go start my busy day. *(He picks up his hat and heads toward the window.)*

HEDDA. You're going through the garden?

BRACK. A shortcut.

HEDDA. The back door.

BRACK. Sometimes the back door can be the most exciting.

HEDDA. Like when someone is firing pistols through it, perhaps?

BRACK. Oh, come now. People don't shoot their favorite old dog, do they?

HEDDA. Never! Especially if it's the only one they've got. *(Brack exits through the French doors. Hedda closes them behind him. She paces around the room, readjusting the chairs around the center table, crosses upstage to the library and retrieves the manuscript. Noise is heard offstage left. Hedda crosses to the desk, places the manuscript in the center drawer and locks it, keeping the key.)*

LOVBORG. *(From offstage.)* I'm telling you, I'm going in. *(He pushes his way in. Berta is behind him. She looks to Hedda, agitated.)*

HEDDA. It's all right, Berta. *(Berta closes the doors.)* A little late to pick up Thea, aren't you, Mr. Lovborg?

LOVBORG. Or early to visit you. Forgive me.

HEDDA. What makes you think she's still here?

LOVBORG. They told me at her hotel she'd been out all night.

HEDDA. Uh-huh.

LOVBORG. Is Tesman awake yet?

HEDDA. I don't think so.

LOVBORG. When did he come home?

HEDDA. Very late.

LOVBORG. Did he tell you anything?

HEDDA. That you'd had a very lively night at Judge Brack's.

LOVBORG. Anything else?

HEDDA. I don't think so. I was half-asleep, so ... *(Mrs. Elvsted enters from the library and crosses to Lovborg.)*

MRS. ELVSTED. Oh, Eilert! Finally!

LOVBORG. Yes. Finally. And too late.

MRS. ELVSTED. What's too late?

LOVBORG. Everything. It's all over for me. I'm finished.

MRS. ELVSTED. Please, don't say that!

LOVBORG. I think you'll say the same thing, when I tell you —

MRS. ELVSTED. Don't tell me anything! I don't want to know.

HEDDA. Maybe you two should be alone? I can leave.

LOVBORG. No, stay. I'd prefer it.

MRS. ELVSTED. I'm telling you, you don't have to say anything.

LOVBORG. I'm not talking about last night.

MRS. ELVSTED. What is it, then — ?

LOVBORG. You and I can no longer see each other, Thea.

MRS. ELVSTED. Not see each other?

HEDDA. Oh, yes. I knew it.

LOVBORG. I no longer have any use for you.

MRS. ELVSTED. No use for me? What are you telling me? That the work we're doing — Don't you want me to help you work?

LOVBORG. I'm not planning on doing any more "work."

MRS. ELVSTED. Then what do I do with myself?

LOVBORG. Just ... try to forget you ever knew me.

MRS. ELVSTED. I can't do that!

LOVBORG. Thea. Try. Go back home.

MRS. ELVSTED. Never! I won't leave you. I won't let you push me away! I have to be by your side when the book comes out!

HEDDA. Ah, yes. The book —

LOVBORG. Yes. Our book. That's what it is.

MRS. ELVSTED. Yes! Our book! Ours! Which is why I have the right to be with you when it comes out! I want the joy of seeing you celebrated! And respected! And honored again! *(Beat.)* I want that joy!

LOVBORG. Thea. Our book is never going to be published.

HEDDA. Ah!

MRS. ELVSTED. Never going to be published?

LOVBORG. It can't be published.

MRS. ELVSTED. Eilert. What have you done with the manuscript?

HEDDA. Yes, the manuscript — ?

MRS. ELVSTED. Where is it?

LOVBORG. Thea. Please don't ask me.

MRS. ELVSTED. I have a right to know! I want to know now!

LOVBORG. I've torn it into a thousand pieces.

MRS. ELVSTED. Oh, no, no — !

HEDDA. But that isn't —

LOVBORG. True? Isn't true? You don't believe me?

HEDDA. All right. If you say so. But it seems so preposterous —

LOVBORG. Nevertheless.

MRS. ELVSTED. You tore up your own book?

LOVBORG. Well, I've torn up my life, so why not do the same to my work?

MRS. ELVSTED. That's what you did last night?

LOVBORG. Yes. You heard me. I tore it into a thousand and one pieces. And tossed them way into the fjord. Far, far out! Into the icy current. *(Beat.)* And then I just watched them ... *(Beat.)* Drift out to sea. And after a while, they'll sink. Deeper and deeper, Thea. *(Beat.)* Just like me. *(Pause.)*

MRS. ELVSTED. Do you know, Eilert — what you've done with the book — It's like you've killed a little child.

LOVBORG. Yes. You're right. It is very much a kind of child killing.

MRS. ELVSTED. How could you? It was my child too!

HEDDA. Ah, the child.

MRS. ELVSTED. Then it is over. Yes. Yes. I'm going, Hedda.

HEDDA. But you're not leaving town, are you?

MRS. ELVSTED. I have no idea what I'm going to do. It's just all ... blackness ahead ... *(She exits.)*

HEDDA. You're not going to see her home, then, Mr. Lovborg?

LOVBORG. Me? Through the streets? You want people to know

she's been with me?

HEDDA. Look. I don't know what happened last night, but is it so completely irrevocable?

LOVBORG. Last night was just the beginning of it. But the beginning of what? I don't have the strength for that kind of life either. I stopped caring. She's actually managed to break my courage, and spirit.

HEDDA. Imagine it. That silly little fool could control someone's destiny. Even so, how could you be so cruel to her?

LOVBORG. It was not cruelty; don't say that!

HEDDA. To destroy the one thing that's consumed her every waking moment for months and years! It seems like cruelty to me.

LOVBORG. Hedda, may I tell you the truth?

HEDDA. Go ahead.

LOVBORG. First, promise me you'll never tell Thea.

HEDDA. You have my word.

LOVBORG. What I told Thea was a lie.

HEDDA. About the manuscript?

LOVBORG. I didn't tear it up. I didn't throw it into the fjord.

HEDDA. So. Then — where — ?

LOVBORG. Destroyed. By me. Nonetheless.

HEDDA. I'm not following you.

LOVBORG. Thea compared me to a child killer ...

HEDDA. Yes. That's what she said.

LOVBORG. But killing his child isn't the worst thing a father can do.

HEDDA. That's not the worst?

LOVBORG. No. I wanted to spare Thea that, at least.

HEDDA. And so then — what is the worst — ?

LOVBORG. Say that a man is out one night — and it's not a good night. It's a wild, totally-out-of-control night. And finally, early in the morning, he crawls home to the mother of his child, and says, "Listen. I've been on this amazing binge. And I took our child with me, and I've lost her. Just lost our child. Somewhere along the way. And who knows where the hell she is, or whose hands she's fallen into ..."

HEDDA. Yes, but it's really only just a book.

LOVBORG. Thea's pure heart and soul were in that book.

HEDDA. I understand that.

LOVBORG. So of course you understand then that she and I can have no future. *(Silence. Hedda tosses the key to the desk drawer lock onto the center table.)*

HEDDA. So what now? What will you do?

LOVBORG. Finish it. Put an end to all of it. The sooner the better.

HEDDA. Listen to me, Eilert Lovborg. If you're going to really do this, do it *courageously.* Do it *gloriously.* Do it right!

LOVBORG. Gloriously? What — with vine leaves in my hair, as you used to say in the old days?

HEDDA. No. No vine leaves. I don't believe in any of that anymore. But gloriously nonetheless. You have to go now, Eilert. *(Beat.)* Don't come back.

LOVBORG. Give George Tesman my love.

HEDDA. Wait! *(She goes to the desk and takes one of her father's revolvers out of the case.)* Do you recognize this? It was aimed at you once.

LOVBORG. You should have used it then.

HEDDA. Here. *(Lovborg takes the revolver and places it in his breast pocket.)* Do it gloriously, Eilert Lovborg. Promise me that. *(She kisses him.)*

LOVBORG. Good-bye, Hedda Gabler. *(He exits. Door slams off-stage. Hedda crosses back to the center table and retrieves the key. She then crosses up to the desk, unlocks the center drawer and pulls out the manuscript. She takes it to the window and begins to read the first page. She looks around and then crosses up to the library to see if anyone is around. She quietly closes the library doors and crosses down to the stove. She kneels at the stove and opens its doors.)*

HEDDA. Now I'm burning your child, Thea! *(She tosses the first few pages into the stove.)* You with your gorgeous hair. Yes! You and Eilert's child! *(More pages go into the fire.)* I'm burning it! I'm burning the child! *(She throws the remainder of the manuscript pages into the fire.)*

# ACT FOUR

*The drawing room is dark. Berta, dressed in black, enters
with a lit oil lamp and sets it on the center table. She lights
it, takes the coffee tray from the center table back into the
library. She reenters, closes the library doors and crosses to the
window to close the drapes. She crosses to the chaise and picks
up the blanket. She then crosses to the stove to place a few logs
on the fire. Hedda is heard offstage in the library playing the
piano. Berta crosses up and opens the library doors.*

*Hedda, also dressed in black, stops playing and spins around
on the piano stool. The doorbell is heard offstage. Berta exits
to answer the door. Hedda rises and crosses down to the stove.
She's about to open the stove doors when Miss Tesman is heard
offstage with Berta. Hedda crosses to the windows and opens
the drapes. Miss Tesman enters.*

MISS TESMAN. Well, Hedda. Here I am, in the colors of sor-
row. My sister's battle is finally over.
HEDDA. As you can see, I've already heard. Tesman sent me a
note.
MISS TESMAN. Yes. He promised he would. But all the same, I
thought I should bring the news of the dead to the house of the
living myself.
HEDDA. That was, as usual, very thoughtful of you.
MISS TESMAN. Oh, but Rina shouldn't have died right now —
this is no time for grief in Hedda's house.
HEDDA. But isn't it a relief that she died peacefully, Miss
Tesman?
MISS TESMAN. Yes! She was so calm at the end. I think it was
seeing George one more time. Being able to say good-bye to him
properly. He hasn't come home yet?

HEDDA. No. He wrote that I shouldn't expect him too soon. But won't you please sit with me for a while?

MISS TESMAN. No, thank you, my dear blessed Hedda. I just don't have the time. I have to get her dressed and prepared so she's buried looking her most beautiful.

HEDDA. Is there nothing I can help you with?

MISS TESMAN. Oh no! Don't even think about it! We can't have Hedda Tesman dwelling on such things — not at a time like this — no!

HEDDA. Oh, but you can't always control your thoughts — they —

MISS TESMAN. Yes, that's the way of the world, isn't it? At my house we'll be sewing a shroud for Rina. And maybe there'll be sewing going on here too, won't there? Of a different kind, thank God. *(Tesman enters.)*

HEDDA. There you are! At last!

TESMAN. Oh, you're here with Hedda, Auntie. Imagine that.

MISS TESMAN. I was just leaving, my dear boy. Well, did you get done all that you promised?

TESMAN. No. I'm afraid I've forgotten half of what I said I'd do! I'll have to come over to you again tomorrow. My brain is just completely blurry today. I can't put my thoughts together.

MISS TESMAN. But George, you mustn't take it this way.

TESMAN. Really? Erh — how — how then?

MISS TESMAN. You have to look carefully. To the center. And find the joy in the midst of your grief. That's what I'm doing.

TESMAN. Oh! Yes, right. You're thinking of Auntie Rina.

HEDDA. It's going to be lonely for you now, Miss Tesman.

MISS TESMAN. For a little while, yes. But not for long, I hope. I don't intend to let Rina's room sit empty.

TESMAN. No? You have someone moving in with you?

MISS TESMAN. There are always people who need to be taken care of.

HEDDA. Do you really want such a burden again?

MISS TESMAN. Burden! Dear God in heaven, child — it's never been a burden for me! Taking care of someone is an honor!

HEDDA. Yes, but at this point, with a stranger — ?

MISS TESMAN. You know? I have a special bond with invalids.

I don't know why. They open up to me. And I to them. And I have to have some reason to live. But maybe you'll need an extra pair of hands here soon...?

HEDDA. Oh, don't think about us, please, really.

TESMAN. But can you imagine what a marvelous time the three of us would have if ...

HEDDA. If — ?

TESMAN. Oh, nothing. I'm sure it'll all take care of itself. Let's hope so. Right? Exactly.

MISS TESMAN. Ah! I think you two have things to talk about — Maybe Hedda has something special to tell you, George. Goodbye! — I have to get to Rina. *(Tesman sees her out. From off-stage.)* Isn't it something? Rina is with me and poor dear Jochum at the same time...!

TESMAN. *(From offstage.)* Yes, that's remarkable, isn't it, darling Aunt Julia! To think! *(Hedda crosses up to the piano and drags a finger across the keys. Tesman returns.)*

HEDDA. It's almost as if you were taking Aunt Rina's death harder than she was.

TESMAN. Oh, it's not just Auntie Rina's death! I'm beside myself worrying about Lovborg.

HEDDA. *(Crossing in to him.)* Any news about him?

TESMAN. I stopped at his hotel to try and tell him his manuscript is safe.

HEDDA. Well? Did you see him?

TESMAN. He wasn't there. And then on the street, I ran into Mrs. Elvsted, who told me that he'd been here early this morning...?

HEDDA. Yes, right after you left.

TESMAN. And — and — did he really say he'd torn up his manuscript?

HEDDA. So he claimed.

TESMAN. But good Lord, he must have been in some sort of dementia! Please tell me you didn't give it to him in that state, Hedda.

HEDDA. No, he didn't get it.

TESMAN. But you did tell him we had it?

HEDDA. No. I did not. Why? Did you say something to Mrs. Elvsted?

TESMAN. No. I didn't think it appropriate. *(Beat.)* But I wish you'd told Eilert. Just think — what if he went out and did something reckless! In his state? Hedda! Give me the manuscript, and I'll take it to him. Where'd you put it?

HEDDA. I no longer have it.

TESMAN. You don't have it? What do you mean by that?

HEDDA. I burned it — every last page. Gone.

TESMAN. Burned it! You burnt Eilert Lovborg's book?

HEDDA. Please don't shout. The maid'll hear you.

TESMAN. But you — ! Burned! Good God, no, no, no! You couldn't have, Hedda! It's impossible!

HEDDA. But true, nevertheless.

TESMAN. Do you have any idea what you've done, Hedda? It's illegal disposal of stolen — lost — property! Think about it! Ask Judge Brack; he'll tell you.

HEDDA. My advice is that it would be best, actually, if you didn't mention it to the Judge, or to anyone else for that matter. Ever.

TESMAN. But what made you think you could do such a horrible thing? I don't understand it! Can you please explain what you were thinking? Answer me! Please!

HEDDA. I did it for your sake, George.

TESMAN. For my sake?

HEDDA. When you came home this morning and told me all about him reading to you —

TESMAN. Yes, what about it?

HEDDA. And you admitted you were envious of his work.

TESMAN. Oh God in heaven, I didn't mean it literally!

HEDDA. Doesn't matter. I couldn't bear the notion of anyone eclipsing you. Ever. Is that clear enough?

TESMAN. Hedda! My God. Is this true? Is this — ? Yes — ? You would? For me? For love? You would do something like that because you love me? I mean — imagine that!

HEDDA. Well, there's more. I suppose I should also tell you that we're going to have — No, no, just ask your Auntie. She'll explain everything.

TESMAN. Oh, I think I'm starting to understand! Hedda! *(He claps his hands.)* Good God — is it really true! Can it be? My God!

HEDDA. Don't shout, please. Really. The maid can hear you.

TESMAN. The maid? It's Berta — I'll go tell her myself.

HEDDA. Oh, I'll die. It's killing me, I'm telling you — it's killing me, all this — !

TESMAN. All this what, Hedda — ?

HEDDA. All this pointless, endless absurdity, George.

TESMAN. But what's absurd? My being happy? Well, all right — I won't say anything to Berta.

HEDDA. Oh, why not? She might as well know too.

TESMAN. No, no, it can wait. But Aunt Julia has to know — and also — you've started calling me "George"! Oh, she'll be so thrilled!

HEDDA. When she hears that I've burnt Eilert Lovborg's manuscript for your sake?

TESMAN. Yes, well, of course we can never say anything about that. But that you have this fire in your heart for me — surely Aunt Julia can be told that! Huh? Perhaps it's a phenomenon of young wives. Do you think? *(Mrs. Elvsted enters.)*

MRS. ELVSTED. Oh, Hedda, please don't be angry with me for coming back again…!

HEDDA. What's happened, Thea?

TESMAN. Has something happened to Eilert?

MRS. ELVSTED. Yes! I'm scared that he's had some sort of accident.

HEDDA. Do you think?

TESMAN. What makes you say that?

MRS. ELVSTED. Because I heard them whispering about him at my hotel when I walked in!

HEDDA. Well, what were they saying?

MRS. ELVSTED. I just got little scraps! They stopped talking when they saw me. And I didn't dare come right out and ask!

TESMAN. Let's hope you misunderstood, Mrs. Elvsted!

MRS. ELVSTED. No — it had to be him they were talking about. I heard them say something about a hospital —

TESMAN. A hospital?

HEDDA. No — that's impossible!

MRS. ELVSTED. I just know, I can tell — something terrible's happened to him.

TESMAN. Hedda, maybe I should go into town and see if I can find out anything?

HEDDA. No! Don't you get mixed up in all this. *(Judge Brack enters. Berta closes the door behind him.)*

TESMAN. Judge. What a surprise!

BRACK. Yes. I had to come see you right away.

TESMAN. I can see that you've heard the news from Aunt Julia.

BRACK. That and more.

TESMAN. It's all so tragic, isn't it? Eh?

BRACK. Well, my dear Tesman, that really depends on how you look at it.

TESMAN. Is there something else?

HEDDA. Another tragedy, Judge?

BRACK. Again, that really depends on how you look at it, Mrs. Tesman.

MRS. ELVSTED. Oh, it's Eilert, isn't it? Something's happened.

BRACK. How did you know, Mrs. Elvsted? Did you hear something?

MRS. ELVSTED. No, no. Nothing at all, but —

TESMAN. Oh, for God's sake, tell us!

BRACK. Well. I'm sorry. But Eilert Lovborg's been taken to the hospital. He's dying.

MRS. ELVSTED. Oh, God, oh God! No!

TESMAN. To the hospital? Dying!

HEDDA. So fast.

MRS. ELVSTED. I have to see him. He thinks I hate him. I have to see him while he's still alive!

BRACK. It won't do any good, Mrs. Elvsted. No one's allowed in.

TESMAN. But what happened to him? Surely he didn't try to do something stupid to himself — ?

HEDDA. Yes. I'm sure that's exactly what he's done.

TESMAN. Hedda — how can you — ?

BRACK. Unfortunately, Mrs. Tesman, you've guessed exactly right.

MRS. ELVSTED. Oh my God, oh, how horrible.

TESMAN. Attempted suicide! Can you imagine?

HEDDA. Shot himself.

BRACK. Right again, Mrs. Tesman.

MRS. ELVSTED. When?

BRACK. This afternoon. Between three and four.

TESMAN. But good God — where did he do it? Eh?

BRACK. I don't know. In his hotel room, I suppose. I only know that he was found shot in the chest.

MRS. ELVSTED. Oh, how horrible!

HEDDA. In the chest you said?

BRACK. Yes.

HEDDA. Oh.

BRACK. Why, Mrs. Tesman?

HEDDA. Nothing.

TESMAN. And he wounded himself critically, you say?

BRACK. Mortally. He's probably already dead.

MRS. ELVSTED. Yes! I can feel it! It's over!

TESMAN. Are you absolutely certain of this?

BRACK. I talked to one of the policemen.

HEDDA. Finally, a bold and decisive act!

TESMAN. Good God, what are you saying, Hedda?

HEDDA. I'm saying that there's glory and beauty in it.

BRACK. Hmn, Mrs. Tesman —

TESMAN. Glory! What an idea — !

MRS. ELVSTED. How can you — ? Where's the beauty in such a savage act?

HEDDA. Eilert Lovborg settled up with himself. He had the courage to do what had to be done. To me that is beautiful.

MRS. ELVSTED. Don't delude yourself into thinking that's how it happened, Hedda! What he did, he did out of madness — delirium!

TESMAN. No. Despair! Complete desperation.

HEDDA. Not at all. Of that, I am completely certain.

MRS. ELVSTED. He must have! Just like when he tore up the book!

BRACK. The manuscript? He tore it up?

MRS. ELVSTED. Yes. Last night.

TESMAN. Oh. Hedda. What are we doing to do?

BRACK. It's so strange.

TESMAN. How horrible. Imagine him. Dying like that. And not to have left behind the one thing that would have given him immortality!

MRS. ELVSTED. If only it could be pieced back together...!

TESMAN. I would give anything if that were possible!

MRS. ELVSTED. Perhaps it can be, Mr. Tesman.

TESMAN. How?

MRS. ELVSTED. *(Pulling a large pile of notes out of her handbag.)* He dictated. I kept the notes. Look. I kept them with me —

TESMAN. *(Crossing to Mrs. Elvsted.)* Oh let me see —

HEDDA. *(Leaning in.)* Ah.

MRS. ELVSTED. They're not in any order, it's just a jumble.

TESMAN. Can you imagine? We could put it in order? Do you think — ? If we helped each other — ?

MRS. ELVSTED. We could at least try.

TESMAN. I know we can do it! We have to do it! I'll put everything I've got into it. Yes! My own research can wait. I have to do it. Hedda, do you understand: I owe it to Eilert's memory.

HEDDA. Perhaps.

TESMAN. All right, Mrs. Elvsted — do you think we can put our heads together and organize all this? *(Beat.)* Mrs. Elvsted? Do you think you can try? I know it's hard just now.

MRS. ELVSTED. I'll do everything I can, Mr. Tesman.

TESMAN. Well then. Let's start. At the beginning. *(He helps her pick up the pile of notes and then leads her upstage toward the library.)* Let's settle ourselves in here. Excuse us, Judge. Come on, Mrs. Elvsted. They exit into the library.

HEDDA. Ah, Judge. What Eilert Lovborg's done — it's an amazing act of liberation!

BRACK. Liberation? I'm sure it was, for him.

HEDDA. I meant for me. Liberating for me. To know that there can actually still be acts of courage in this world. Something that literally shimmers with beauty.

BRACK. Oh my dear Hedda ...

HEDDA. Oh, I know what you're going to say, because finally, after all is said and done, you're really sort of a specialist too, aren't you? Just like — yes! You can admit it to me.

BRACK. I can see Eilert Lovborg meant more to you than you have ever been willing to admit — even to yourself — or is that a misapprehension on my part?

HEDDA. I'm not even going to respond to such a question. From you. All I will say is that Eilert Lovborg had the courage to live the life he wanted. As he wanted. And was brave enough to end it gloriously. And then walk away from the party when it stopped shimmering and glowing. Even though it was still early.

BRACK. As much as it pains me, Hedda, I am going to have to divest you of your romantic little illusion.

HEDDA. Illusion?

BRACK. One that would have been shattered soon enough anyway.

HEDDA. What do you mean?

BRACK. He didn't shoot himself in quite the glorious way you imagine.

HEDDA. No?

BRACK. No. I wasn't being entirely forthright in my description of events.

HEDDA. What did you leave out?

BRACK. For the sake of poor Mrs. Elvsted, I did a little selective editing here and there.

HEDDA. Where, exactly?

BRACK. First. He's already dead.

HEDDA. He died at the hospital?

BRACK. Right. Without regaining consciousness.

HEDDA. What else did you leave out?

BRACK. It didn't happen in his hotel room, either.

HEDDA. Well. That's not important, is it…?

BRACK. It is. Only in that he was actually found in the boudoir of one Madame Diana.

HEDDA. That's impossible! He wouldn't have gone back there today!

BRACK. He was there this afternoon. Ranting about something he claimed they'd stolen from him. Going on incomprehensibly about a lost child —

HEDDA. Ahh. That's what it was!

BRACK. I had at first presumed he was talking about the manuscript, but I hear now that he destroyed that himself, so maybe it was his journal.

HEDDA. I suppose. And that's where he did it?

BRACK. Yes. The pistol in his breast pocket. One round discharged. The bullet wound was absolutely horrible.

HEDDA. Yes. A bullet in the chest.

BRACK. Much lower, actually. *(Beat.)* Below the stomach.

HEDDA. That too! It's funny — it's comedy, isn't it? This curse of mine — everything I touch turns ugly and absurd!

BRACK. There's another ugly aspect to this, Hedda. *(Beat.)* The pistol he was carrying —

HEDDA. Well! What about it!

BRACK. He must have stolen it.

HEDDA. No, that's not true, he didn't.

BRACK. There's no other possibility, really. He had to have — Shhh!

TESMAN. *(From offstage.)* Hedda! *(Tesman and Mrs. Elvsted enter from the library.)* Hedda, the light's so bad in there. You know?

HEDDA. Yes, I'm sure it is.

TESMAN. Could we perhaps work in here?

HEDDA. Of course. That's fine. *(She crosses up to the desk and removes the revolver case.)* No! Wait! Let me ... clear some space ...

TESMAN. Oh, don't bother, Hedda.

HEDDA. *(Taking the revolver case up into the library.)* I'll put all of this in here. *(She lays the case on the piano and then returns. Tesman and Mrs. Elvsted set themselves up to work at the desk.)* Well, dear Thea, are you getting anywhere with Eilert's memorial?

MRS. ELVSTED. Oh God, I don't know how we're going to be able to make sense of it all.

TESMAN. We'll find our way through it all. Besides — it's the thing I do best: collating other people's papers. *(Hedda crosses to Judge Brack, who is downstage.)*

HEDDA. *(Softly.)* What did you say about the pistol?

BRACK. *(Also quietly.)* That he must have stolen it.

HEDDA. Why "stolen"?

BRACK. It's the only explanation.

HEDDA. Right.

BRACK. He had been here this morning, hadn't he?

HEDDA. Yes.

BRACK. Were you alone with him?

HEDDA. Briefly.

BRACK. Did you leave the room while he was here?

HEDDA. No.

BRACK. Think about it. Didn't you leave, for just a second?

HEDDA. I went into the hall. For just a second.

BRACK. And where was your pistol case?

HEDDA. I had put it away —

BRACK. Had you? Really?

HEDDA. It was on the writing table.

BRACK. And have you checked to see if both pistols are there?

HEDDA. No.

BRACK. No need to. I saw the pistol Lovborg used. And I recognized it immediately.

HEDDA. Do you, by any chance, have it?

BRACK. The police have it.

HEDDA. What will they do with it?

BRACK. Try and trace it to the owner.

HEDDA. Will they succeed?

BRACK. No, Hedda Gabler. Not as long as I don't say anything.

HEDDA. And if you did say something?

BRACK. Ah. Then — you would claim it was stolen.

HEDDA. I'd rather die.

BRACK. Ahh! We say these things, but never really mean them, do we?

HEDDA. And what if it turns out that the gun hadn't been stolen? And the owner were found — then what?

BRACK. There would be a scandal.

HEDDA. A scandal...!

BRACK. Uh-huh. *(Beat.)* The kind of intensely public scandal you're so terrified of. You would have to go to court. You and Madame Diana. She would have to explain how the whole thing happened. Step by step. Was it an accident? Was it murder? Was he trying to pull the gun out of his pocket to threaten her with? Was there a struggle? Did she grab the gun from his hand and shoot him with it? Then put the gun back into his pocket? It's possible. She's a strong woman, Madame Diana. And quite, quite capable.

HEDDA. None of that repulsive business has anything to do with me.

BRACK. No. But you'll have to answer the question: Why did you give Eilert Lovborg the gun? *(Beat.)* And — and — what conclusions will people draw from the shocking fact that you did give it to him?

HEDDA. That's true. I hadn't thought of that.

BRACK. Well, luckily there's no danger. As long as I keep quiet.

HEDDA. So in other words: I'm in your power. From now on.

BRACK. Dearest Hedda — believe me — I never abuse my power.

HEDDA. All the same. I'm in your power. Dependent on your will. Essentially — your prisoner. Not free! Still! I can't do it, I just can't stand it.

BRACK. Realistically — one learns to tolerate the inevitable. Adjusting isn't really all that hard.

HEDDA. Maybe. Perhaps. *(Turning upstage and crossing up to Tesman and Mrs. Elvsted.)* Well, George? How's the big project, eh?

TESMAN. Oh, God, it'll be absolute months of work! Literally months!

HEDDA. Imagine that! Amazing! Extraordinary! *(She runs her hands lightly through Mrs. Elvsted's hair.)* Isn't it strange, Thea? To be sitting here with Tesman just the way you used to sit with Eilert?

MRS. ELVSTED. Oh, if only I could inspire your husband the same way.

HEDDA. Oh, I'm sure you will, in time.

TESMAN. You know what, Hedda? I do think that's true! I really do! But you go back and talk to the Judge.

HEDDA. Can't I be of any use at all?

TESMAN. No, none at all. *(Turning downstage to Brack.)* May I leave Hedda in your care for a bit, Judge? So she's not bored? If you don't mind?

BRACK. Oh. Nothing could give me more pleasure.

HEDDA. *(Smiling.)* Thank you. But I'm so tired. I'm worn down. I'll just go in the other room and rest for a little while.

TESMAN. Yes, dear, you do that ... Hmn ... *(Hedda crosses up into the library and closes the doors behind her. Tesman and Mrs. Elvsted go back to work on the notes. Brack takes a seat at the center table. Wild piano music starts up in the library.)*

MRS. ELVSTED. Oh! What's she doing?

TESMAN. *(Running to the library doors.)* Hedda — my darling — I don't think this is the time for that. *(He opens the library doors. Hedda is revealed playing the piano.)* Think of Aunt Rina! Not to

76

mention Eilert!

HEDDA. *(From over her shoulder as she plays.)* Yes, and Aunt Julia. And everyone else. *(She stops playing and turns on the stool to face Tesman.)* I'll be very quiet from now on, I promise you. *(Hedda closes the library doors again. Tesman returns to the desk.)*

TESMAN. It can't make her very happy, seeing us do this awful work, can it? Maybe the thing to do is have you move into Aunt Julia's and we can work there.

MRS. ELVSTED. Yes, maybe that would be the best plan.

HEDDA. *(From offstage.)* I can hear what you're saying, Tesman! And what do you expect me to do stuck out here?

TESMAN. Oh, I'm sure Judge Brack will be kind enough to visit.

BRACK. Of course, Mrs. Tesman. I'll be right here.

HEDDA. *(From offstage.)* You can always hope, Judge, can't you? To be top dog? *(A shot is heard from within.)*

TESMAN. *(As he goes to the library doors.)* There she goes, playing with her pistols again. *(Tesman opens the doors to reveal Hedda dead draped across the piano keyboard. Berta enters through the hallway door. Tesman starts to pick Hedda up.)* Oh, my God! She's shot herself. *(He drags her downstage toward the window.)* She's shot herself in the head.

BERTA and MRS. ELVSTED. *(Screaming.)* Oh, my God!

TESMAN. I can't believe it.

BRACK. God in heaven! People — people — don't do such things.

## End of Play

# PROPERTY LIST

Logs
Letter
Manuscript
Blanket
Flowers with card (BERTA)
Suitcase (TESMAN)
Package of slippers (MISS TESMAN)
Slip of paper (MRS. ELVSTED)
Slippers (TESMAN)
Pistol (HEDDA)
Revolver case (HEDDA)
Journals, books (TESMAN)
Photo album (HEDDA)
Cigarette (TESMAN)
Tray of punch, punch glasses, biscuits (TESMAN)
Lamp (BERTA)
Coffee service on tray (BERTA)
Hat (JUDGE)
Key (HEDDA)
Notes, handbag (MRS. ELVSTED)

# SOUND EFFECTS

Doorbell
Gunshot
Bell
Piano music
Noise
Door slam

# NEW PLAYS

★ **AT HOME AT THE ZOO by Edward Albee.** Edward Albee delves deeper into his play THE ZOO STORY by adding a first act, HOMELIFE, which precedes Peter's fateful meeting with Jerry on a park bench in Central Park. "An essential and heartening experience." *–NY Times.* "Darkly comic and thrilling." *–Time Out.* "Genuinely fascinating." *–Journal News.* [2M, 1W] ISBN: 978-0-8222-2317-7

★ **PASSING STRANGE book and lyrics by Stew, music by Stew and Heidi Rodewald, created in collaboration with Annie Dorsen.** A daring musical about a young bohemian that takes you from black middle-class America to Amsterdam, Berlin and beyond on a journey towards personal and artistic authenticity. "Fresh, exuberant, bracingly inventive, bitingly funny, and full of heart." *–NY Times.* "The freshest musical in town!" *–Wall Street Journal.* "Excellent songs and a vulnerable heart." *–Variety.* [4M, 3W] ISBN: 978-0-8222-2400-6

★ **REASONS TO BE PRETTY by Neil LaBute.** Greg really, truly adores his girlfriend, Steph. Unfortunately, he also thinks she has a few physical imperfections, and when he mentions them, all hell breaks loose. "Tight, tense and emotionally true." *–Time Magazine.* "Lively and compulsively watchable." *–The Record.* [2M, 2W] ISBN: 978-0-8222-2394-8

★ **OPUS by Michael Hollinger.** With only a few days to rehearse a grueling Beethoven masterpiece, a world-class string quartet struggles to prepare their highest-profile performance ever—a televised ceremony at the White House. "Intimate, intense and profoundly moving." *–Time Out.* "Worthy of scores of bravissimos." *–BroadwayWorld.com.* [4M, 1W] ISBN: 978-0-8222-2363-4

★ **BECKY SHAW by Gina Gionfriddo.** When an evening calculated to bring happiness takes a dark turn, crisis and comedy ensue in this wickedly funny play that asks what we owe the people we love and the strangers who land on our doorstep. "As engrossing as it is ferociously funny." *–NY Times.* "Gionfriddo is some kind of genius." *–Variety.* [2M, 3W] ISBN: 978-0-8222-2402-0

★ **KICKING A DEAD HORSE by Sam Shepard.** Hobart Struther's horse has just dropped dead. In an eighty-minute monologue, he discusses what path brought him here in the first place, the fate of his marriage, his career, politics and eventually the nature of the universe. "Deeply instinctual and intuitive." *–NY Times.* "The brilliance is in the infinite reverberations Shepard extracts from his simple metaphor." *–TheaterMania.* [1M, 1W] ISBN: 978-0-8222-2336-8

**DRAMATISTS PLAY SERVICE, INC.**
440 Park Avenue South, New York, NY 10016  212-683-8960  Fax 212-213-1539
postmaster@dramatists.com  www.dramatists.com

# NEW PLAYS

★ **AUGUST: OSAGE COUNTY by Tracy Letts.** WINNER OF THE 2008 PULITZER PRIZE AND TONY AWARD. When the large Weston family reunites after Dad disappears, their Oklahoma homestead explodes in a maelstrom of repressed truths and unsettling secrets. "Fiercely funny and bitingly sad." *–NY Times.* "Ferociously entertaining." *–Variety.* "A hugely ambitious, highly combustible saga." *–NY Daily News.* [6M, 7W] ISBN: 978-0-8222-2300-9

★ **RUINED by Lynn Nottage.** WINNER OF THE 2009 PULITZER PRIZE. Set in a small mining town in Democratic Republic of Congo, RUINED is a haunting, probing work about the resilience of the human spirit during times of war. "A full-immersion drama of shocking complexity and moral ambiguity." *–Variety.* "Sincere, passionate, courageous." *–Chicago Tribune.* [8M, 4W] ISBN: 978-0-8222-2390-0

★ **GOD OF CARNAGE by Yasmina Reza, translated by Christopher Hampton.** WINNER OF THE 2009 TONY AWARD. A playground altercation between boys brings together their Brooklyn parents, leaving the couples in tatters as the rum flows and tensions explode. "Satisfyingly primitive entertainment." *–NY Times.* "Elegant, acerbic, entertainingly fueled on pure bile." *–Variety.* [2M, 2W] ISBN: 978-0-8222-2399-3

★ **THE SEAFARER by Conor McPherson.** Sharky has returned to Dublin to look after his irascible, aging brother. Old drinking buddies Ivan and Nicky are holed up at the house too, hoping to play some cards. But with the arrival of a stranger from the distant past, the stakes are raised ever higher. "Dark and enthralling Christmas fable." *–NY Times.* "A timeless classic." *–Hollywood Reporter.* [5M] ISBN: 978-0-8222-2284-2

★ **THE NEW CENTURY by Paul Rudnick.** When the playwright is Paul Rudnick, expectations are geared for a play both hilarious and smart, and this provocative and outrageous comedy is no exception. "The one-liners fly like rockets." *–NY Times.* "The funniest playwright around." *–Journal News.* [2M, 3W] ISBN: 978-0-8222-2315-3

★ **SHIPWRECKED! AN ENTERTAINMENT—THE AMAZING ADVENTURES OF LOUIS DE ROUGEMONT (AS TOLD BY HIMSELF) by Donald Margulies.** The amazing story of bravery, survival and celebrity that left nineteenth-century England spellbound. Dare to be whisked away. "A deft, literate narrative." *–LA Times.* "Springs to life like a theatrical pop-up book." *–NY Times.* [2M, 1W] ISBN: 978-0-8222-2341-2

**DRAMATISTS PLAY SERVICE, INC.**
440 Park Avenue South, New York, NY 10016  212-683-8960  Fax 212-213-1539
postmaster@dramatists.com  www.dramatists.com